Late-Medieval German Women's Poetry: Secular and Religious Songs

Library of Medieval Women

ISSN 1369–9652

Series Editor: Jane Chance

The Library of Medieval Women aims to make available, in an English translation, significant works by, for, and about medieval women, from the age of the Church Fathers to the fifteenth century. The series encompasses many forms of writing, from poetry, visions, biography and autobiography, and letters, to sermons, treatises and encyclopedias; the subject matter is equally diverse: theology and mysticism, classical mythology, medicine and science, history, hagiography, and instructions for anchoresses. Each text is presented with an introduction setting the material in context, a guide to further reading, and an interpretive essay.

We welcome suggestions for future titles in the series. Proposals or queries may be sent directly to the editor or publisher at the addresses given below; all submissions will receive prompt and informed consideration.

Professor Jane Chance, Department of English, MS 30, Rice University, PO Box 1892, Houston, TX 77251–1892, USA. E-mail: jchance@rice.edu

Boydell & Brewer Limited, PO Box 9, Woodbridge, Suffolk, IP12 3DF, UK. E-mail: boydell@boydell.co.uk Website: www.boydellandbrewer.com

Previously published titles in this series appear at the back of this book

Late-Medieval German Women's Poetry: Secular and Religious Songs

**Translated from the German
with Introduction, Notes and Interpretive Essay**

Albrecht Classen
University of Arizona

D. S. BREWER

PT
1160
. E8
.C55
2004

First published 2004
D. S. Brewer, Cambridge

ISBN 1 84384 021 9

D. S. Brewer is an imprint of Boydell & Brewer Ltd
PO Box 9, Woodbridge, Suffolk IP12 3DF, UK
and of Boydell & Brewer Inc.
PO Box 41026, Rochester, NY 14604–4126, USA
website: www.boydellandbrewer.com

A CIP catalogue record for this book is available
from the British Library

Library of Congress Cataloging-in-Publication Data
Late-Medieval German women's poetry : secular and religious songs : translated from the
German with introduction, notes and interpretive essay / Albrecht Classen.
    p. cm. – (Library of medieval women, ISSN 1369–9652)
  Includes bibliographical references and index.
  ISBN 1–84384–021–9 (hardback : alk. paper)
  1. German poetry – Early modern, 1500–1700 – Translations into English.   2. Christian
poetry, German – Early modern, 1500–1700 – Translations into English.   3. Songs, German
– Germany – 15th century – Translations into English.   4. Songs, German – Germany –
16th century – Translations into English.   5. Women poets, German – Early modern,
1500–1700.   6. German poetry – Women authors – History and criticism.   7. Christian
poetry, German – Early modern, 1500–1700 – History and criticism.   I. Classen, Albrecht.
II. Title.   III. Series.
PT1156.L38 2004
831′.30809287–dc22

2004000084

This publication is printed on acid-free paper

Printed in Great Britain by
Antony Rowe Ltd, Chippenham,Wiltshire

Contents

Introduction

Contrary to common opinion, during the Middle Ages and the early-modern age a substantial number of aristocratic and other women were actively involved in composing literary texts. On the one hand, we know that some major female writers treated primarily worldly matters, particularly in the French-speaking area, examples being the *troubairitz* (courtly love poets), Marie de France, and Christine de Pizan. On the other, women such as Hildegard of Bingen, Mechthild of Magdeburg, Marguerite Porete, Bridget of Sweden, Caterina of Siena, Julian of Norwich, and Margery Kempe expressed themselves in writing and gained public recognition through mysticism. This religious phenomenon was not limited to one specific country, though the majority of mystical writers seem to have emerged in Germany during the thirteenth and fourteenth centuries.

Nevertheless, despite these promising indications of a flourishing literature by women, throughout Europe, the world of the courts allowed little, if any room for women poets, except for Marie de France and Christine de Pizan. In particular, the history of medieval German literature is almost entirely dominated by male writers, as the female mystics were practically the only ones who came forward as writers, were mostly recognized publicly, and had their visions recorded and so preserved for posterity. Perhaps these are the reasons why currently it seems as if research on medieval and early-modern German women writers has come almost to a standstill as no new names have been noted, and no new texts have been explored for several decades. Scholarship reports of no female courtly poets who composed erotic love poetry (*Minnesang*), courtly romances, or didactic texts, and the currently available evidence suggests that active women were essentially limited to the religious area.[1]

---

[1] To remedy this deplorable situation, I have collected and translated most of the relevant texts from that period in *Frauen in der deutschen Literaturgeschichte. Die ersten 800 Jahre*, Women in German Literature, 4 (New York: Lang, 2000); amazingly, when a woman identifies herself in a didactic text, such as the Winsbeckin, even feminist scholars tend to discard her contribution to German literature because of the poet's traditional, almost patriarchal attitudes about gender relations, reconfirming the norms of male society: see Ann Marie Rasmussen, *Mothers and Daughters in Medieval German Literature* (Syracuse: Syracuse University Press, 1997), 136–59. For an example representative of the

Traditionally, two responses existed to deal with this situation: either to accept the current assessment of the absent woman's voice during the German Middle Ages, except the mystical writers, or to begin a new search in the literary archives. To provide weight to the second, often neglected option, this book will offer English translations of a vast corpus of women's heretofore ignored poetic texts from the late Middle Ages and the sixteenth century.[2]

It is disappointing that currently few noteworthy efforts in German literary scholarship have expanded our current perspectives on secular medieval women writers. Consequently, the purpose of the present volume is to provide new stimulation for renewed efforts in this direction. The theoretical, practical, and political reasons are manifold: after decades of intensive critical struggles to win recognition for a few outstanding historical figures, most closely connected with the Church, modern scholarship has adopted a small but important group of primarily mystical women writers who occupy their own niche, albeit to some extent marginal, and yet, as we have recently recognized, also central to medieval culture.[3] The literary texts by these female poets span the period from the tenth through to the fifteenth century, the traditional time frame of the Middle Ages.[4] The discovery of these historical

---

little progress and lack of innovative perspective in the exploration of medieval German women's literature, see *Schwierige Frauen—schwierige Männer in der Literatur des Mittelalters*, ed. Alois M. Haas and Ingrid Kasten (Bern: Peter Lang, 1999). Kerstin Merkel and Heide Wunder, eds., *Deutsche Frauen der Frühen Neuzeit. Dichterinnen, Malerinnen, Mäzeninnen* (Darmstadt: Primus, 2000), include chapters on such well-known figures as Caritas Pirckheimer (Ursula Hess), Catharina Regina von Greiffenberg (Lynne Tatlock), Anna Ovena Hoyers (Cornelia Niekus Moore), and Elisabeth von der Pfalz (Christine van den Heuvel); but the editors also invited several contributors to discuss outstanding women painters, architects, and art collectors—all of whom lived in the seventeenth and eighteenth centuries, at a time when the situation for women had improved considerably anyway.

2   For previous attempts in this direction, see Albrecht Classen, ed., *Women as Protagonists and Poets in the German Middle Ages*, Göppinger Arbeiten zur Germanistik, 528 (Göppingen: Kümmerle, 1991); ibid. and Peter Dinzelbacher, "Weltliche Literatur von Frauen des Mittelalters," *Mediaevistik* 8 (1995): 55–73. For the Middle Ages in general, see Peter Dronke, *Women Writers of the Middle Ages. A Critical Study of Texts from Perpetua († 203) to Marguerite Porete († 1310)* (Cambridge: Cambridge University Press, 1984); *The Writings of Medieval Women. An Anthology*, 2nd ed., translations and introductions by Marcelle Thiébaux, The Garland Library of Medieval Literature (New York and London: Garland, 1994).

3   Albrecht Classen, "Worldly Love—Spiritual Love. The Dialectics of Courtly Love in the Middle Ages," *Studies in Spirituality* 11 (2001): 166–86; for a historical perspective, see Peter Dinzelbacher, "Religiöse Frauenbewegung und städtisches Leben im Mittelalter," *Frauen in der Stadt*, ed. Günther Hödl, Fritz Mayrhofer, and Ferdinand Opll (Linz: Österreichischer Arbeitskreis für Stadtgeschichtsforschung, 2003), 229–64.

4   Spanish Germanists have also begun to explore the literary contributions by medieval German women writers: see Eva Parra Membrives, *Mundos femeninos emancipados*.

personalities and critical analyses of their works have satisfied the modern interest in medieval women's voices, for feminist literary historians can now claim a stake in the history of medieval German literature, rather than deferring to the canon of male writings, as was mostly done until the 1960s and 1970s.

To establish a basis for subsequent investigations and translations, let us briefly review contributions by those medieval women writers from the Middle Ages who have left a noticeable impact and have often been included in the literary canon. I will also sketch an outline of the current status of German literary research on women's contributions during that time to understand more clearly the context of the women's songs introduced here.

The Abbess Hrotsvit of Gandersheim (935–after 973) composed remarkable Latin religious narratives, dramas, and short epics. Her dramas especially continue to appeal to a modern sense of what truly constitutes literature and offer a considerable degree of entertainment—surprisingly refreshing for convent literature. In addition to their obvious religious messages, they are filled with violent actions, comic features, obscene allusions, and intriguing highly self-conscious and independently minded women characters.[5] Although her dramas seem to have found a wider readership in other convents throughout Germany, her texts were nevertheless soon forgotten until 1497 when the famous Humanist Conrad Celtis rediscovered them in the St. Emmeram monastery in Regensburg.

Abbess Hildegard of Bingen (1098–1179) authored powerful visionary texts, political letters, scientific treatises on herbal medicine, gynecology, human sexuality, and also religious poems, all in Latin. In addition, she created a considerable corpus of liturgical songs. Hildegard was highly praised as the "Sibyl of the Rhine" and generally esteemed as a major figure during what Charles Haskins coined the "Twelfth-Century Renaissance" in 1927.[6] She personally addressed

---

Reconstrucción teóretico-empírica de una propuesta literaria femenina en la Edad Media alemana, Textos de Filología, 5 (Zaragoza: Anubar, 1998).

[5] See the excellent selection and translation by Katharina Wilson, *Hrotsvit of Gandersheim: A Florilegium of her Works*, trans. with Introduction, Interpretive Essay and Notes, Library of Medieval Women (Cambridge: D. S. Brewer, 1998).

[6] Charles H. Haskins, *The Renaissance of the Twelfth Century* (1927; rpt. New York: New American Library, 1972); see also Heinrich Fichtenau, *Heretics and Scholars in the High Middle Ages, 1000–1200*, trans. Denise A. Kaiser (University Park: The Pennsylvania State University Press, 1998, orig. 1992); C. Stephen Jaeger, *The Envy of Angels. Cathedral Schools and Social Ideals in Medieval Europe, 950–1200*, Middle Ages Series (Philadelphia: University of Pennsylvania Press, 1994); Peter Damian-Grint, *The New Historians of the Twelfth-Century Renaissance. Inventing Vernacular Authority* (Woodbridge: The Boydell Press, 1999).

popes and emperors, and traveled throughout Germany preaching to the masses, although women were usually excluded from such pastoral activities.[7] The inclusa (hermit) Lady Ava (d. 1127) from the area of Melk, Austria, was the first woman writer to resort to Middle High German when she paraphrased large sections of the New Testament in poetic form. Her texts are not only religious in content, and repeatedly she addresses her audience as well and briefly reflects upon her own life.[8] Her near contemporary Abbess Herrad of Hohenburg in Alsace (d. 1195), and her teacher Abbess Relindis (d. 1169), wrote a famous Latin encyclopedical *Hortus Deliciarum* (The Garden of Delights), a collection of text excerpts from classical (ancient) authors including about sixty poems from renowned twelfth-century male writers. Elisabeth of Schönau (1129–1164), a Benedictine nun in the convent of Schönau near Trier, was strongly influenced by Hildegard of Bingen with whom she corresponded intensively. Her mystical visions, edited and copied down by her brother Ekbert, have come down to us in a large number of manuscripts, which were mostly written in Latin, reflecting widespread interest in her experiences and writings. They were translated into Middle High German in later centuries.[9]

The true heyday of medieval German women's literature, however, did not begin until the thirteenth century, when mystical writers such as Gertrud the Great (1256–1301/02),[10] Mechthild of Hackeborn (1241/1242–1299),[11] and Mechthild of Magdeburg (ca. 1208–1282/

7   Beverly Sian Rapp, "A Woman Speaks: Language and Self-Representation in Hildegard's Letters," *Hildegard of Bingen. A Book of Essays*, ed. Maud Burnett McInerney, Garland Medieval Casebooks (New York and London: Garland, 1998), 3–24; see also Alain Boureau, *The Myth of Pope Joan*, trans. (from the French) by Lydia G. Cochrane (Chicago and London: The University of Chicago Press, 2001), 195–202.

8   Ernst Ralf Hintze, *Learning and Persuasion in the German Middle Ages*, Garland Studies in Medieval Literature, 15 (New York and London: Garland, 1997); *Ava's New Testament Narratives. "When the Old Law Passed Away"*, Introduction, Translation, and Notes by James A. Rushing, Jr., Medieval German Texts in Bilingual Editions, II (Kalamazoo, MI: Medieval Institute Publications, 2003).

9   Anne L. Clark, *Elisabeth of Schönau. A Twelfth-Century Visionary*, Middle Ages Series (Philadelphia: University of Pennsylvania Press, 1992); Ekbert emphasizes: "I . . . have written down all these things and others which are gathered from her revelations in such a way that where the words of the angel were Latin I left them unchanged, but where they were in German, I translated them into Latin, as clearly as I could, adding nothing from my own presumption . . . " (52).

10 See, for example, Gertrud von Helfta, *Exercitia spiritualia. Geistliche Übungen. Lateinisch und deutsch*, ed., trans. and with commentary by Siegfried Ringler (Elberfeld: Humberg, 2001).

11 Margarete Hubrath, *Schreiben und Erinnern. Zur "memoria" im Liber Specialis Gratiae Mechthilds von Hackeborn* (Paderborn, Munich, Vienna, and Zürich: Ferdinand Schöningh, 1996).

1297)[12]—all nuns in the cloister of Helfta near Eisleben (today in Sachsen-Anhalt)—emerged as major writers of visionary accounts, the former two in Latin, the latter in Middle Low German. Many other nuns followed their examples, particularly in Southwest Germany where whole convents strove to experience mystical visions, leading to the creation of so-called "Sister-Books": large collections of mystical accounts by most members of the respective convents.[13] Other women writers, such as Margarethe Ebner in Medingen (near Dillingen), Christine Ebner and Adelheid Langmann in Engelthal, Sister Irmgard in Kirchberg, and Elsbeth of Oye (Oetenbach), produced significant "auto-biographical" writings enriched with many poems, prayers, medita-tions, letters and responses from their friends.[14]

When we turn to the fifteenth century, three major female figures, who strongly deviated from the religious tradition, deserve our atten-tion: Elisabeth of Nassau-Saarbrücken (after 1393–1456), Eleonore of Austria (ca. 1433–1480), and Helene Kottanner(in) (ca. 1400–after 1470).[15] The first two, from the upper echelons of the aristocracy, are well-known for their translations of French courtly romances into German, whereas the latter produced the first personal memoirs in the history of German literature, recounting her personal experiences as a

---

[12] Mechthild of Magdeburg, *The Flowing Light of the Godhead*, trans. and introduced by Frank Tobin, Preface by Margot Schmidt (New York and Mahwah: Paulist Press, 1998).

[13] Gertrud Jaron Lewis, *By Women, for Women, about Women. The Sister-Books of Fourteenth-Century Germany*, Studies and Texts, 125 (Toronto: Pontifical Institute of Mediaeval Studies, 1996); Rebecca L. R. Garber, *Feminine Figurae. Representations of Gender in Religious Texts by Medieval German Women Writers, 1100–1375*, Studies in Medieval History and Culture, 10 (New York and London: Routledge, 2003).

[14] A fairly large number of medieval German women's songs have also come down to us, but they were primarily, if not entirely, written by male poets who used the female voice to enrich their poetic repertoire: see *Frauenlieder des Mittelalters*, bilingual, trans. and ed. Ingrid Kasten (Stuttgart: Reclam, 1990); see also Hubert Heinen, "The Woman's Songs of Hartmann von Aue," *Vox Feminae. Studies in Medieval Women's Songs*, ed. John F. Plummer (Kalamazoo, MI: Medieval Institute Publications, 1981), 95–110; *The Voice of the Trobairitz. Perspectives on the Women Troubadours*, ed. William D. Paden (Philadelphia: University of Pennsylvania Press, 1989); *New Images of Medieval Women. Essays toward a Cultural Anthropology*, ed. Edelgard DuBruck, Mediaeval Studies, 1 (Lewiston, Queenston, and Lampeter: Edwin Mellen Press, 1989); see also Anne L. Klinck and Ann Marie Rasmussen, eds., *Medieval Woman's Song: Cross-Cultural Approaches*, The Middle Ages Series (Philadelphia: University of Pennsylvania Press, 2002).

[15] Ursula Liebertz-Grün, "Höfische Autorinnen. Von der karolingischen Kulturreform bis zum Humanismus," *Deutsche Literatur von Frauen*, Vol. 1: *Vom Mittelalter bis zum Ende des 18. Jahrhunderts*, ed. Gisela Brinker-Gabler (Munich: Beck, 1988), 40–64; for brief introductions and modern German translations, see Albrecht Classen, *Frauen in der deutschen Literaturgeschichte. Die ersten 800 Jahre*, Women in German Literature, 4 (New York: Lang, 2000). See also Maya Bijvoet Williamson, *The Memoirs of Helene Kottanner (1439–1440)*, trans. from the German with Introduction, Interpretative Essay and Notes (Cambridge: D. S. Brewer, 1998).

chamber maid for the German Empress Elizabeth, wife of Albrecht II. In particular, she reports that after Elizabeth had been widowed, she asked Helene to secure the Hungarian crown for her yet unborn son and hence for the Hapsburg family. The author describes in astonishing detail and in lively manner how she managed to steal (!) the crown from the Hungarian nobles and secretly transport it to her lady just in time for the delivery of her son. Consequently this male heir to the throne meant that Elizabeth did not have to marry the Polish King Wladislaus III, selected by the Hungarian nobles for her.[16]

Undoubtedly, this short catalogue of names already represents a remarkable collection of female voices in medieval Germany, but none composed any significant courtly romances or secular love poetry, as far as we can tell today. There are two exceptions, fifteenth-century writers Elisabeth of Nassau-Saarbrücken and Eleonore of Austria. But both worked primarily as translators rendering French verse romances into late-medieval German prose, which led scholars to disregard them as authentic poets.[17] However, most medieval literature could be categorized as 'translation' as only very few texts are truly original and are not based on any sources, such as Wolfram of Eschenbachs's unique though fragmentary *Titurel*. Medieval aesthetics held that rewriting and remodeling older traditions were more valuable than creating original narratives.[18]

To date we know of no German woman writer who could be compared with the tenth- and eleventh-century Old Norse Skáldonur and to the twelfth-century Old Occitan *troubairitz* poets; we also seek in vain for a

---

[16] *Die Denkwürdigkeiten der Helene Kottannerin (1439–1440)*, Wiener Neudrucke, 2 (Vienna: Österreichischer Bundesverlag, 1971).

[17] Reinhold Hahn, *Von frantzosischer zungen in teütsch: das literarische Leben am Innsbrucker Hof des späteren 15. Jahrhunderts und der Prosaroman Pontus und Sidonia (A)*, Mikrokosmos, 27 (Frankfurt a.M.: Peter Lang, 1990); remarkably, only seven years later he had changed his opinion entirely and now unequivocally acknowledges Eleonore's authorship as if there were no doubt or question: Eleonore von Österreich, *Pontus und Sidonia*, ed. Reinhard Hahn, Texte des späten Mittelalters und der frühen Neuzeit, 38 (Berlin: Schmidt, 1997), 12.

[18] Albrecht Classen, "Women in 15th-Century Literature: Protagonists (Melusine), Poets (Elisabeth von Nassau-Saarbrücken), and Patrons (Mechthild von Österreich)," *"Der Buchstab tödt – der Geist macht lebendig". Festschrift zum 60. Geburtstag von Hans-Gert Roloff*, ed. James Hardin and Jörg Jungmayr, vol. I (Bern, Berlin, Frankfurt a.M.., et al.: Lang, 1992), 431–58; for the medieval concept of the poet as translator, see Carl Lofmark, "Der höfische Dichter als Übersetzer," *Probleme mittelhochdeutscher Erzählformen*, ed. Peter F. Ganz and Werner Schröder (Berlin: E. Schmidt, 1972), 40–62; Albrecht Classen, "Deutsch-französische Literaturbeziehungen im 15. Jahrhundert: 'Volksbücher' als Übersetzungen oder authentische Werke?," *New Texts, Methodologies, and Interpretations in Medieval German Literature (Kalamazoo Papers 1992–1995)*, ed. Sibylle Jefferis, Göppinger Arbeiten zur Germanistik, 670 (Göppingen: Kümmerle, 1999), 173–207.

female writer of Middle High German literature comparable to the famous Anglo-Norman Marie de France (ca. 1170–1200) or the outspoken French "feminist" Christine de Pizan (1364–1429?).[19] Disappointingly, at present it is impossible even to locate major secular and vernacular female authors throughout the entire Middle Ages. Perhaps we simply do not know of them because their texts might be lost today, or perhaps women were indeed not empowered to participate in the public discourse on courtly love. To put it differently, our quest for the female voice in the Middle Ages has, with a few exceptions, not yet succeeded despite intriguing indicators such as the enormous literary output of mystical visionaries. Perhaps more women have created literary texts than modern literary histories have acknowledged.[20]

In other words, apart from the unique history of medieval French literature in which we know of at least two major female writers,[21] medieval European women did not emerge as significant authors of courtly romances and poetry. Suggestions that a large number of anonymously preserved texts which could have been composed by female writers, or that some male names of courtly love poetry represent pseudonyms for female poets need investigation. To date we only know that women indeed did not write such texts, as we can only observe that no such texts have come down to us as far as archival research has confirmed. Nevertheless, as the subsequent translation of fifteenth- and sixteenth-century German women's poetry will demonstrate, results depend very much on research methods, investigative and

[19] See also the thirteenth-century Florentine poet La Compiuta Donzella, from whom three sonnets have survived, "A la stagion che il mondo foglia e fiora," "Lasciar voría lo mondo e Dio servire," and "Ornato di gran pregio e di valenza," see Neda Jeni, "La Compiuta Donzella," *An Encyclopedia of Continental Women Writers*, ed. Katharina M. Wilson, vol. 1 (New York and London: Garland, 1991), 327–28; for an edition, see *Poeti del duecento. Poesia cortese toscana e settentrionale, Tomo secondo: A cura di Gianfranco Contini* (1960; Milano and Napoli: Giulio Einaudi, 1976), 248–52; the most recent study seems to be by Paola Malpezzi Price, "Uncovering Women's Writings: Two Early Italian Women Poets," *Journal of the Rocky Mountain Medieval and Renaissance Association* 9 (1988): 1–15.

[20] Bea Lundt, ed., *Auf der Suche nach der Frau im Mittelalter. Fragen, Quellen, Antworten* (Munich: Fink, 1991); for a current status report, see Birgit Kochskämper, "Die germanistische Mediävistik und das Geschlechtsverhältnis. Forschungen und Perspektiven," *Germanistische Mediävistik*, ed. Volker Honemann and Tomas Tomasek, 2nd rev. ed. (Münster: Lit Verlag, 2000), 309–52; Susan Boynton, "Women's Performance of the Lyric before 1500," *Medieval Woman's Song*, 47–65.

[21] Angelika Rieger, *Trobairitz. Der Beitrag der Frau in der altokzitanischen höfischen Lyrik. Edition des Gesamtkorpus*, Beihefte zur Zeitschrift für Romanische Philologie, 233 (Tübingen: Niemeyer, 1991); Marie de France, *Lais*, ed. Alfred Ewert with an Introduction and Bibliography by Glyn S. Burgess, French Texts Series (Bristol: Bristol Classical Press, 1995); Charity Cannon Willard, *Christine de Pizan. Her Life and Works* (New York: Persea Books, 1984).

selection criteria, and perception of what constitutes, in the first place, women's literature. To quote Edward Hallett Carr who wisely ruminated about the historian's role, which can be well adapted here for our own purposes: literary history "is a continuous process of interaction between the [literary] historian and his [her] facts, an unending dialogue between the present and the past."[22]

Because previous decades were less interested in women's writing, scholars did not seek them out, whereas today, Feminism, by now transformed into Gender Studies, and influenced by poststructuralist thinking, has fundamentally changed our view of women in the premodern era. Again in Carr's terms: "The past is intelligible to us only in the light of the present; and we can fully understand the present only in the light of the past."[23] In other words, modern realization of the significant roles that women have always played in any society leads us to re-examine what we really know about women's lives and specifically their literary contributions during the (German) Middle Ages.

Recent scholarship

Literary histories of medieval German women writers published since around 1985 have provided a detailed outline of all those female authors known today. Subsequently, however, scholarship has contented itself with this canon of women authors outlined above, most members of religious convents, and only few closely connected with worldly, courtly society. Let us first consider the most significant example, *Frauen Literatur Geschichte*, edited by Hiltrud Gnüg and Renate Möhrmann (1985).[24] Gnüg and Möhrmann rightly claimed that their book represented the first attempt to provide a broad overview of German women's literary creativity throughout times. But they also warned about deceptive expectations as the history of women's writing was not characterized by continuity, regular growth, or a linear development, as might have been the case for the history of men's writing. According to Gnüg and Möhrmann, women's literature has regularly witnessed serious collapses and often could not rely on any solid long-term traditions, except, perhaps, mystical writings. Consequently, women have rarely been able to establish literary groups, circles, or schools of thought because they were mostly excluded from public life until at least the middle of the twentieth

---

[22] Edward Hallett Carr, *What is History?* (New York: Vintage Books, 1961), 35.
[23] Carr, *What is History?*, 69.
[24] Gnüg, Hiltrud, Renate Möhrmann, eds., *Frauen, Literatur, Geschichte: schreibende Frauen vom Mittelalter bis zur Gegenwart*, 2nd, completely revised and expanded, ed. (Stuttgart: Metzler, 1999; orig. 1985).

century. In other words, women's literature tends to be written by individuals who follow their own paths and do not imitate or copy each other.

Although many mystical writers have gained in respect through modern literary scholarship, no women writers have ever achieved acclaim comparable to that enjoyed by the monumental male figures of the classical period in the history of medieval German literature (ca. 1170–ca. 1220), such as Hartmann of Aue, Walther von der Vogelweide, Heinrich of Morungen, Wolfram of Eschenbach, and Gottfried of Strassburg. This also applies, alas, to the later centuries, if not to the entire period until the seventeenth and eighteenth centuries, when finally women were accepted widely and slowly made their voices heard in public, gaining greater recognition. To illustrate this point more dramatically, we all know of Chrétien de Troyes, Wolfram of Eschenbach, Dante Alighieri, Giovanni Boccaccio, Francis Petrarch, and Geoffrey Chaucer; but even outstanding women writers such as Hildegard of Bingen or Caterina da Siena do not seem comparable to them. Moreover, the latter two represent entirely different literary orientations, purposes, styles, and hence also public roles in comparison to their male contemporaries.

The first two chapters of *Frauen Literatur Geschichte* focus on the Middle Ages. In the first chapter, Margret Bäurle and Luzia Braun discuss German mystical writers Hildegard of Bingen and Mechthild of Magdeburg, offering brief comparison with Catherine of Genoa, Angela of Foligno, and Theresa of Avila. Ursula Liebertz-Grün contributes a chapter on women writers at the court, focusing, however, mostly on the Occitan troubairitz (writing in the South of France, Provence), the Anglo-Norman writer Marie de France, and Christine de Pizan. Although Liebertz-Grün remarks that women in medieval Germany were almost entirely mute, she briefly mentions two fifteenth-century translators, Elisabeth of Nassau-Saarbrücken and Eleonore of Austria, leaving the history of mystical literature to subsequent authors Christel Meier and Ursula Peters. The last paragraphs of Liebertz-Grün's examination present several other authors such as Helene Kottannerin who created the earliest memoirs in the history of German literature; from here the author surprisingly introduces three women writers from the early Reformation period, Katharina Zell, Ursula Weyden, and Argula of Grumbach. In the face of these and other similarly remarkable contributions Liebertz-Grün's claim that medieval German women had been almost entirely mute is strongly contradicted by her evidence for the history of sixteenth-century German literature.

In 1999, Gnüg and Möhrmann published a vastly expanded and completely revised second edition, but a careful comparison of both editions reveals that at least for the Middle Ages—with only one exception—practically no new viewpoints or new materials were considered or made available. Liebertz-Grün slightly expands her discussion of Elisabeth of Nassau-Saarbrücken, Eleonore of Austria, and Helenne Kottannerin, and adds a short paragraph on Margarethe of Austria, nominal governor of the Netherlands and member of the Hapsburg family, who was mostly active as a patron and as a letter writer (in French), not to mention those poems which she composed in French. The editors' claim, however, to have prepared a completely revised and expanded edition, does not hold true for the medieval period covered in their book. In other words, despite the second revised edition, no new knowledge about medieval German women writers has been presented to the scholarly community. We are practically still dealing with the same corpus of medieval female literature as it had been outlined first by Lotte Traeger in 1934 and by Peter Dronke in 1984.[25] Since then literary research has probed deeper into these texts, has explored their significant cultural context, religious meaning, and their mystical messages. Nevertheless, research on medieval women authors continues to spin the same wheels, basically accepting the traditional viewpoint that medieval German literature was by and large entirely dominated by male writers.

A somewhat brighter situation seems to emerge in the literary history edited by Gisela Brinker-Gabler, *Deutsche Literatur von Frauen* (1988).[26] Again Ursula Liebertz-Grün examined the Middle Ages, but her observations and discussions prove almost identical to those in her previously published chapter on the same topic. The exceptions are that at least a few new names are incorporated. The Merovingian Queen Dhuoda, for instance, who wrote a didactic text for her son William in Latin in 841,[27] is mentioned as a very early example of women's contributions, followed by the same canon of high-medieval French and late-medieval German women writers considered in Gnüg's and Möhrmann's volume. For instance, the paragraph on Margarethe of Austria is basically a verbatim copy of the one included in the 1999

[25] Lotte Traeger, "Das Frauenschrifttum in Deutschland von 1500–1650" (Ph.D. Prague 1934); Traeger's study, though today hardly known among modern scholars, represents highly impressive research and deserves to be published because of the outstanding breadth and depth of her expertise; see also Peter Dronke, *Women Writers of the Middle Ages.*

[26] Gisela Brinker-Gabler, *Deutsche Literatur von Frauen. Vom Mittelalter bis zur Gegenwart,* 2 vols. (Munich: Beck, 1988).

[27] *Handbook for William. A Carolingian Woman's Counsel for her Son by Dhuoda,* trans. and with an Introduction by Carol Neel (Washington, DC: The Catholic University of America, 1991).

edition of *Frauen Literatur Geschichte*. Fortunately, other contributors, such as Wiebke Freytag, Christel Meier, and Ursula Hess broaden the perspectives on a considerably wider spectrum of German women writers. Freytag, for instance, discusses the Anglo-Saxon Nun Hugeburc, the Ottonian Abbess Hrotsvith of Gandersheim, the eleventh-century anchorite Frau Ava, and the twelfth-century Abbess Herrad of Hohenburg. Christel Meier, on the other hand, focuses entirely on Hildegard of Bingen, briefly examining her impact on Gebeno of Eberbach and Elisabeth of Schönau. Finally, Liebertz-Grün contributes a lengthy chapter on Dutch, German, and French mystical writers from the thirteenth through the fifteenth centuries.

The arrival of the Renaissance north of the Alps also meant that individual women authors, such as Magdalia, wife of Erasmus of Rotterdam, the Nuremberg Abbess Charitas Pirckheimer, the learned Margarete Peutinger, wife of the famous Augsburg humanist, historian, and collector Conrad Peutinger, and her daughter Juliana, became involved in public debates. These women are duly recorded in *Deutsche Literatur von Frauen*, but they do not challenge the overall impression that even fifteenth- and sixteenth-century women writers were generally marginalized and that they had to carve out their own niche, never fully achieving the same public status as their male contemporaries.[28]

Ursula Hess, who authored the chapter on German Renaissance women, offers a solid overview of scholarship published until the late 1980s, but she definitely moves into the world of *latinitas* (learned texts written exclusively in Latin), concluding with an extensive presentation of the Italian Olympia Fulvia Morata. Morate, who taught Greek at the University of Heidelberg, was an anomaly in many respects because women were excluded from the university and were rarely taught Latin, much less Greek, a language generally unknown to medieval Europe. However, if we accept women writers into the canon of German literature from the early and high Middle Ages who wrote in Latin, such as Hrotsvith of Gandersheim and Hildegard of Bingen, the same compromise has to be accepted for the late Middle Ages.

---

[28] Hanna-Barbara Gerl, *Einführung in die Philosophie der Renaissance*, Die Philosophie (Darmstadt: Wissenschaftliche Buchgesellschaft, 1989), 28–31, with an extensive bibliography. Curiously, international Renaissance scholars generally ignore or disregard the contributions by German Renaissance women writers: see Ann Rosalind Jones, *The Currency of Eros. Women's Love Lyric in Europe, 1540–1620*, Women of Letters (Bloomington and Indianapolis: Indiana University Press, 1990); *Die Frau in der Renaissance*, ed. Paul Gerhard Schmidt, Wolfenbütteler Abhandlungen zur Renaissanceforschung, 14 (Wiesbaden: Harrassowitz, 1994); now see Kerstin Merkel and Heide Wunder, eds., *Deutsche Frauen der Frühen Neuzeit*.

Finally, Barbara Becker-Cantarino discusses the last phase of the medieval period with a chapter on women writers during the Protestant Reformation, focusing on Katharina Zell, Argula of Grumbach, Elisabeth of Brunswick-Lüneburg, and Anna Ovena Hoyers. The same figures also appear in Becker-Cantarino's seminal monograph, *Der lange Weg zur Mündigkeit. Frau und Literatur (1500–1800)* (1987), where she adds, however, the name of Ursula of Münsterberg to the canon, before she abruptly turns to the seemingly more productive seventeenth century, closing the chapter on the Middle Ages definitely for good.[29] But recently Merry Wiesner-Hanks and Joan Skocir have successfully widened our perspective by including hitherto unknown and newly discovered women authors active during the time of the Reformation into their collection *Convents Confront the Reformation* (1996), to which we now have to add Gertrud Angermann's edition of Anna of Quernheim's (before 1525–1590) religious poetry.[30]

Since the late 1980s, many efforts to chart and deepen the history of medieval German women's literature have been made, especially documented by massive modern encyclopedias and lexica on continental women writers and their social conditions, such as those by Katharina M. Wilson (1991), Helen Tierney (1989–1991), and Ute Hechtfischer, Renate Hof, Inge Stephan, and Flora Veit-Wild (1998).[31] Unfortunately, most of these efforts were marred by insufficient research, outdated information, and inadequate critical acumen. Publication of these encyclopedias, however, indicates that the establishment of a canon of women's literature has been completed, prodding readers to turn their

[29]   Barbara Becker-Cantarino, *Der lange Weg zur Mündigkeit. Frau und Literatur (1500–1800)* (Stuttgart: Metzler, 1987).

[30]   Merry Wiesner-Hanks, *Convents Confront the Reformation: Catholic & Protestant Nuns in Germany*, introduced and ed. by Merry Wiesner-Hanks, trans. by Joan Skocir and Merry Wiesner-Hanks, Reformation Texts with Translation (1350–1650), 1 (Milwaukee: Marquette University, 1996); Gertrud Angermann, *Anna von Quernheim (vor 1520–1590). Die erste bekannte Liederdichterin Westfalens und 25 ihrer geistlichen Gesänge in niederdeutscher Sprache* (Bielefeld: Aisthesis Verlag, 1996); see now Barbara Becker-Cantarino, "Renaissance oder Reformation? Epochenschwellen für schreibende Frauen und die Mittlere Deutsche Literatur," *Das Berliner Modell der Mittleren Deutschen Literatur. Beiträge zur Tagung Kloster Zinna 29.9.–01.10. 1997*, ed. and introduced by Christiane Caemmerer, Walter Delabar, et al., Chloe, 33 (Amsterdam and Atlanta: Editions Rodopi, 2000), 69–87.

[31]   Katharina M. Wilson, ed., *An Encyclopedia of Continental Women Writers*, 2 vols. (New York and London: Garland, 1991); Helen Tierney, ed., *Women's Studies Encyclopedia*, 3 vols. (New York, Westport, CT, and London: Greenwood Press, 1989–1991); Ute Hechtfischer, Renate Hof, Inge Stephan, and Flora Veit-Wild, eds., *Metzler Autorinnen Lexikon* (Stuttgart and Weimar: Metzler, 1998); see also Katharina M. Wilson, Paul Schlueter, and June Schlueter, eds., *Women Writers of Great Britain and Europe. An Encyclopedia*, Garland Reference Library of the Humanities, 1980 (New York and London: Garland, 1997).

attention from the treasure houses of the medieval archives to the edited texts. This has certainly triggered a new wave of interpretations; but full understanding of the true scope of medieval German women's literature remains obscure, unless we naively accept the current status of research, adding no further major female writers to our canon.[32]

For instance, the well-known *Dictionary of Literary Biography*, in its volume on the German High Middle Ages, edited by James Hardin and Will Hasty (1994),[33] includes only one woman writer, Mechthild of Magdeburg. The subsequent volume, edited by James Hardin and Max Reinhart, covering the period from 1280–1580 (1997), includes the names of Elisabeth of Nassau-Saarbrücken, Argula of Grumbach, Olympia Fulvia Morata, and Caritas Pirckheimer, that is, four litteratae (female writers) compared to thirty-six litterati (male writers).[34]

Undoubtedly, scholarship on medieval women has established a solid text basis, especially for mystical literature,[35] but the legitimate concern to establish a fully recognized corpus of medieval German women writers has also precluded the logical further search for hitherto unknown female authors since the struggle to establish a canon automatically leads to closure and disregard of any further voices. Certainly, many efforts have been made to understand particular aspects of mystical texts,[36] coupled with outstanding editorial and translation work,[37] and accompanied by detailed research.[38] But the search for active

---

[32] An example of reliable research is provided by *Women Writers of Great Britain and Europe*, ed. Wilson, Schlueter, and Schlueter. *Medieval Women. An Encyclopedia*, ed. Katharina M. Wilson and Nadia Margolis (Westport, CT: Greenwood Publishing, 2004), promises to be an exemplary collaborative effort by scholars and editors.

[33] James Hardin and Will Hasty, eds., *German Writers and Works of the High Middle Ages: 1170–1280*, Dictionary of Literary Biography, 1038 (Detroit, Washington, DC, and London: Gale Research, 1994).

[34] James Hardin and Max Reinhart, eds., *German Writers of the Renaissance and Reformation 1280–1580*, Dictionary of Literary Biography, 139 (Detroit, Washington, DC, and London: Gale Research, 1997).

[35] Elizabeth Alvilda Petroff, *Medieval Women's Visionary Literature* (New York and Oxford: Oxford University Press, 1986); Albrecht Classen, ed., *Women as Protagonists and Poets in the German Middle Ages. An Anthology of Feminist Approaches to Middle High German Literature*, Göppinger Arbeiten zur Germanistik, 528 (Göppingen: Kümmerle, 1991); Peter Dinzelbacher, *Mittelalterliche Frauenmystik* (Paderborn, Munich, Vienna, and Zurich: Schöningh, 1992).

[36] Prudence Allen, RSM, *The Concept of Women*, Vol. II: *The Early Humanist Reformation* (Grand Rapids, MI, and Cambridges Eerdmans Leuven: Peeters, 2002), 31–64.

[37] Mechthild von Magdeburg's *Flowing Light*, trans. Tobin (New York and Mahwah: Paulist Press, 1998).

[38] Kurt Ruh, *Frauenmystik und franziskanische Mystik der Frühzeit*, Geschichte der abendländischen Mystik, II (Munich: Beck, 1993), 1993; Elizabeth Andersen, *The Voices of Mechthild of Magdeburg* (Oxford, Bern, et al.: Lang, 2000); Hildegard Elisabeth Keller, *My Secret is Mine* (*Studies on Religion and Eros in the German Middle Ages*, 2001).

women writers of the German Middle Ages and the early-modern age has not led to any significant new insights about the cultural-historical conditions of women and has yielded no names of any new medieval women writers, if they existed in the first place.[39] It almost seems as if the liberating effect of research on mysticism also resulted in a remarkable stifling of new investigative approaches as to what other sources of medieval literature might tell us about actual contributions by women authors who have hitherto remained unknown to us.[40]

The current situation in medieval feminism

Since the 1980s, a centuries-old impression of women's mostly subdued role in German medieval literature has been questioned and opened to investigation. The new catchword 'Gender Studies' has triggered the latest wave of research, but the various attempts to lift the veil covering women's true literary history have been mostly abandoned in favor of theoretical investigations pertaining to gender roles, re-examining traditional forms of allegedly female writings, and questions of generic origin.[41] The only noteworthy exception currently seems to be medieval and early-modern women's mystical literature which is vigorously studied from many different perspectives.[42]

---

[39] Bea Lundt, ed., *Auf der Suche*; most recently I discovered the cookbook by Anna Wecker (late sixteenth century) in the Herzog August Library, Wolfenbüttel (HAB 7.1 Oec), along with a nuptial song by her (HAB 177 Quod. [24]). Very little is currently known about her, but the available archival materials promise to yield more information. I am in the process of preparing an edition and will investigate Wecker's life and work in greater detail.

[40] How much work remains to be done is well illustrated by the case of the mystical Beguine Agnes Blannbekin (d. 1315): see Ulrike Wiethaus, *Agnes Blannbekin, Viennese Beguine: Life and Revelations*, trans. from the Latin with Introduction, Notes and Interpretive Essay, Library of Medieval Women (Cambridge: D. S. Brewer, 2002); see also my critical assessment, "Writing a History of German Women's Literature from the Middle Ages to the Present: Problems and New Approaches," *German Studies Review* XXIII, 1 (2000): 13–31.

[41] Ingrid Bennewitz and Helmut Tervooren, eds., *Manlîchiu wîp, wîplîch man. Zur Konstruktion der Kategorien 'Körper' und 'Geschlecht' in der deutschen Literatur des Mittelalters*, Beihefte zur Zeitschrift für deutsche Philologie, 9 (Berlin: Schmidt, 1999). The contributors offer many interesting and valuable perspectives on women figures within canonical texts by male writers and on female mystical literature, but none of them introduces any new names or makes a serious attempt to view medieval German women's literature strictly from a feminist perspective. Instead, this certainly noteworthy volume reconfirms the canon, instead of breaking open its barriers.

[42] See, for example, Johannes von Magdeburg, OP, *Die Vita der Margareta contracta, einer Magdeburger Rekluse des 13. Jahrhunderts*, ed. for the first time by Paul Gerhard Schmidt, Studien zur katholischen Bistums- und Klostergeschichte, 36 (Leipzig: Benno-Verlag, 1992); *New Trends in Feminine Spirituality: The Holy Women of Liège and their Impact*, ed. Juliette Dor, Lesley Johnson, and Jocelyn Wogan-Browne (Turnhout, Belgium: Brepols, 1999); Thomas of Cantimpré, *The Life of Christina the Astonishing*, Latin text with facing English translations, trans. Margot King with assistance from David Wiljer (Toronto: Peregrina Publishing, 2nd ed. 1999).

This disconcerting situation needs to be addressed by way of new research, new critical approaches, new criteria by which to evaluate what constitutes women's literature and literature per se in the medieval context, and especially by new archival research—both the medieval manuscript and the early-modern print promise a rich harvest particularly for women's literature if approached from the right perspective. Joan Ferrante, for one, has successfully shaken the stifling walls of traditional feminist research in her wake-up call in *To the Glory of Her Sex* (1997), offering fresh evidence as to how much medieval women could be in control of their own lives and exert power over their countries; she also opens our eyes to hitherto vastly neglected literary genres particularly appealing to women writers in premodern times, such as the letter (epistolarity).[43] Indeed, many medieval women, and German women writers especially, resorted to the letter as a private means of communication and utilized the written word to express their thoughts and feelings. To what degree a letter can be counted as a literary work of art will always have to be determined case by case, but certainly numerous documents demonstrate that epistolary writing, as a creative act, was fully accessible to medieval women, and a surprisingly large number of noble, but also urban ladies resorted to this medium to gain access to the written word, not to speak of the extensive epistolary exchanges among convent women.

Undoubtedly, women in the German Middle Ages did not have an equal share of public power, and they were certainly not in the same position as their male contemporaries to equally contribute to the literary discourse. Nevertheless, as research in female patronage and sociological research on women's hidden political and cultural power have demonstrated, much of our present understanding of women's history depends on the types of questions we ask, on the scholarly approaches we pursue in our research, and how we search for women's representatives of the past.[44]

---

[43] Joan M. Ferrante, *To the Glory of her Sex. Women's Roles in the Composition of Medieval Texts* (Bloomington and Indianapolis: Indiana University Press, 1997); see also Albrecht Classen, " . . . und sie schrieben doch: Frauen als Schriftstellerinnen im deutschen Mittelalter," *Wirkendes Wort* 44, 1 (1994): 7–24; ibid., "Female Exploration of Literacy: Epistolary Challenges to the Literary Canon in the Late Middle Ages," *Disputatio* 1: *The Late Medieval Epistle* (1996): 89–121; however, Ferrante seems not to have taken note of earlier studies on female epistolarity: see, for instance, Albrecht Classen, "Female Epistolary Literature from Antiquity to the Present," *Studia Neophilologica* 60 (1988): 3–13; ibid., "Frauenbriefe an Bonifatius: Frühmittelalterliche Literaturdenkmäler aus moderner mentalitätsgeschichtlicher Sicht," *Archiv für Kulturgeschichte* 72, 2 (1990): 251–73; Janina Cünnen, *Fiktionale Nonnenwelten. Angelsächsische Frauenbriefe des 8. und 9. Jahrhunderts*, Anglistische Forschungen, 287 (Heidelberg: Universitätsverlag C. Winter, 2000).

[44] Jennifer Carpenter and Sally-Beth MacLean, eds., *Power of the Weak. Studies on Medieval Women* (Urbana and Chicago: University of Illinois Press, 1995); June Hall McCash, ed., *The Cultural Patronage of Medieval Women* (Athens and London: The University of Georgia

New avenues?

The present book is based on my own work over the last ten to fifteen years which has been focused on addressing some of these burning desiderata, on expanding our understanding of medieval German women's literature, and on discovering new writers from that time period. Such discoveries are only possible in specialized archives and libraries. Fortunately I have been successful in my endeavors several times while doing research in Germany. One of the best archives particularly for the Reformation period, proved to be the Herzog August Bibliothek (HAB) in Wolfenbüttel. Most of the secular women songs, however, I discovered in the Deutsches Volkslied Archiv (DVA) in Freiburg. My research on religious women's songs gained the most from holdings in the Staatsbibliothek Göttingen. Excellent research opportunities also exist in the Staats- und Universitätsbibliothek Bremen, not to mention the large number of other major collections such as those at the Universitätsbibliothek Leipzig and the Universitätsbibliothek Marburg. But the basic principle of all research on medieval women's literature consists in the patient and diligent investigations of large and small archival holdings all over Germany, as this quest concerns an almost entirely unexplored field. It involves the constant reexamination of what truly constitutes literature and what genres women might have resorted to for their own issues and interests. Should we resort rather to a purely text- and discourse-related definition? What genres might women have relied on for their own issues and interests?

To explain how the present volume of women's songs came about, a brief outline of my own investigations might be appropriate. First, while doing research at the Herzog August Bibliothek Wolfenbüttel, I (re)discovered a surprisingly large number of Reformation women writers, such as Argula of Grumbach, Katharina Zell, die Graserin, Charitas Pirckheimer, etc. Most (but certainly not all) of these figures have been discussed for some time now in greater detail, as we have seen above, but the full scope of their writing will remain a mystery until critical editions of all of their texts have been published.[45] Recently, as a first step, I have

Press, 1996); Lesley Smith and Jane H. M. Taylor, eds., *Women and the Book. Assessing the Visual Evidence* (London, Toronto and Buffalo: The British Library, University of Toronto Press, 1997).

[45] Albrecht Classen, "Frauen in der deutschen Reformation: Neufunde von Texten und Autorinnen sowie deren Neubewertung," *Die Frau in der Renaissance*, ed. Paul Gerhard Schmidt, Wolfenbütteler Abhandlungen zur Renaissanceforschung, 14 (Wiesbaden: Harrassowitz, 1994), 179–201; Hermina Joldersma, "Argula von Grumbach," *German Writers of the Renaissance and Reformation, 1280–1580*, Dictionary of Literary Biography, 179 (Detroit, Washington, DC, and London: Gale Research, 1997), 89–96; Barbara Becker-Cantarino, "Renaissance oder Reformation?," discusses the well-known writers Caritas

included excerpts from some of their writings in my textbook *Frauen in der deutschen Literaturgeschichte* (2000), adapting them slightly for modern German readers. Simultaneously, I began another major research project on late-medieval German songbooks, the result of which was a monograph introducing the reader to this extensive genre.[46] During my work on these huge collections of popular songs, I discovered a surprisingly large number of secular love songs composed by women poets. Their anonymity, however, meant I had to rely on the context, the poems' language, and the statements clearly marked by female interests.[47] To proceed further and to reach more solid ground, I began to explore religious songbooks and made two noteworthy discoveries. First, many late-medieval female convents were extraordinary, extensive centers of the arts and literature. Even though the nuns generally did not compose their own religious hymns, but copied them from previous song collections created by male poets (monks and other clerics). Consequently, we should also consider the copying process as an important contribution to the history of late-medieval German literature.[48] Copying proves to be more than simply transferring word for word, instead it mostly involves a recreation process relying on the original model which then is transformed into a new text by the translator or copyist.

Second, numerous Protestant church songbooks (sixteenth century) contained some, or even many, songs composed by women, who until recently were entirely unknown to modern scholarship. Although the content and language of these songs do not reveal, as far as I can tell, many gender-specific features, most are identified by names, either written down at the end of the song, or hidden in the song as acrostics.[49]

About the texts
To make this hitherto unknown treasure of women's lyric poetry available to an English-speaking audience, I have selected a number of

---

Pirckheimer, Argula von Grumbach, Anna Ovena Hoyers, and then moves into the seventeenth century.

[46] *Frauen in der deutschen Literaturgeschichte. Die ersten 800 Jahre. Ein Lesebuch*, selection, trans. und commentary by A. Classen, Women in German Literature, 4 (New York: Peter Lang, 2000); ibid., *Deutsche Liederbücher des 15. und 16. Jahrhunderts*, Volksliedstudien, 1 (Münster and New York: Waxmann, 2001).

[47] Albrecht Classen, *Deutsche Frauenlieder des 15. und 16. Jahrhunderts*, Amsterdamer Publikationen zur Sprache und Literatur, 136 (Amsterdam and Atlanta: Editions Rodopi, 1999); for a critical review with very constructive suggestions, see Judith P. Aikin, in *Daphnis* 28, 2 (1999).

[48] Jeffrey Hamburger, *Nuns as Artists. The Visual Culture of a Medieval Convent* (Berkeley, Los Angeles, London: University of California Press, 1997).

[49] Albrecht Classen, *'Mein Seel fang an zu singen'. Religiöse Frauenlieder des 15.–16. Jahrhunderts*, Studies in Spirituality Supplement (Leuven: Peeters, 2002).

secular and religious songs from both of my previous editions, and translated them into English. This selection will, I hope, undermine the misconception that the history of medieval and early-modern German literature was almost totally dominated by male writers, bearing in mind remarkable women mystical writers such as Hildegard of Bingen (Latin), Mechthild of Magdeburg (Low German), Mechthild of Hackeborn and Gertrud the Great (Latin), not to mention the two fifteenth-century secular women writers, Elisabeth of Nassau-Saarbrücken and Eleonore of Austria, and their contemporary Helene Kottannerin (early-modern German). This English translation of secular and religious songs by German women poets will establish new grounds for the study of continental medieval and early-modern women writers, with an emphasis on German women's literature. For instance, although Ann Rosalind Jones focused her research entirely on English, Spanish, French, and Italian women poets from the sixteenth and early seventeenth centuries,[50] she and other feminist scholars now might widen their perspectives to include German secular and religious songs as well. The *Female Autograph*, as Domna C. Stanton calls it, can now also be identified within German-speaking lands.[51] The present English translation of those songs will make their texts available to a wider audience, providing international research on medieval women with new literary material with which to explore the literary accomplishments of medieval and early-modern women writers in German-speaking lands.

The chosen time-frame will extend the medieval period to at least 1600, but in terms of women's literary history this is a negligible extension of the chronological period, especially since the traditional periodization (Middle Ages versus Reformation) has been questioned by recent historians and theological scholars.[52] My translation will provide innovative insights into a female tradition developed especially in the sixteenth century. Then future researchers might trace further into the past: we already know of such outstanding women writers as Hrotsvith of Gandersheim (tenth century) and Frau Ava (eleventh–twelfth century) but, although their texts are the only ones preserved in writing,

---

[50] Ann Marie Jones, *The Currency of Eros. Women's Love Lyric in Europe, 1540–1620* (Bloomington and Indianapolis: Indiana University Press, 1990).

[51] *Female Autograph: Theory and Practice of Autobiography from the Tenth to the Twentieth Century*, ed. Domna C. Stanton (Chicago and London: The University of Chicago Press, 1984).

[52] See the contributions to *Normative Centering*, ed. Rudolf Suntrup and Jan R. Veenstra, Medieval to Early Modern Culture, 2 (Frankfurt a.M., Berlin, et al.: Peter Lang, 2002), especially Berndt Hamm's article, "Normative Zentrierung im 15. und 16. Jahrhundert. Beobachtungen zu Religiosität, Theologie und Ikonologie," 21–63.

they might not have been the only women writers of their time. Writers contemporary with the prolific creation of secular and religious songs in the fifteenth and sixteenth centuries might then come to light for the high and even early Middle Ages if we return to archival research equipped with new theoretical concepts, methodologies, and an improved sensitivity to gender issues.

It is possible that the curious phenomenon of the song "Dû bist mîn, ich bin dîn" by a Tegernsee nun from ca. 1180, today included in the famous edition *Des Minnesangs Frühling*, might come to be considered not an exception or an aberration, but rather part of a tradition that has yet to be identified.[53] Most scholars have disregarded the possibility that this song could have been composed by a nun for a number of philological reasons, and because of its highly erotic nature. But the newly emerging tradition of women's love poetry and religious songs from the fifteenth and sixteenth centuries, if properly understood as literary analogy, will offer fresh support for the hypothesis of female authorship of this very early and highly impressionistic love poem.

Many of the secular love songs offered in the first part of the translation represent rather difficult cases because they have come down to us anonymously and often fail to meet the same expectations as do the poems by male contemporaries. I address these questions in the interpretive essay that follows the translation, considering why these songs belong to the category of women's songs and how they might be evaluated within the context of late-medieval and early-modern literature. In certain cases the female voice seems nothing but a mask for a male poet; in others, evidence for female authorship is solid. Further, all secular songs represent popular poetry and were not composed for and by humanists or other intellectuals. The religious songs that comprise the second part of the translation are by a surprisingly large number of clearly identifiable, but heretofore ignored, women poets with specifically religious orientations, mostly from the sixteenth century. Whereas the secular love poems challenge us in many respects and require a very careful approach in identifying them as gender-specific, religious songs reflect a very different situation. Here we face fewer problems in identifying the historical personalities, but more as to what extent, if any, these songs address female issues. Does a religious content provide room for a woman poet to express her own concerns? Can religious experiences be couched in specifically female images or language? What religious themes interested female poets, and what did they try to achieve

---

[53] See my *Frauen in der deutschen Literaturgeschichte*, 66f.

with their poetry? These questions will be addressed in the interpretive essay.

The selection of songs is derived from the entire region of German-speaking lands, laying the foundation for future research on female poets from ca. 800 to ca. 1600. On the basis of this selection, however, we can already affirm that many women joined the more or less public discourse on love and contributed to various popular genres of "Volkslieder" (folk songs) and religious songs. The latter were mostly composed by women in the Protestant areas and have been preserved in many different church songbooks. Although the secular love songs have only been preserved anonymously, their exceptional character can easily be recognized. Whereas most popular songs composed by male poets are identified as such, either through a reference to the poet's profession, social status, or educational background, women's songs almost always address specific female concerns and reflect women's interest in love. When a male poet utilizes the mask of female speaker, his strategy is apparent, as in the case of No. 3 (Ambras No. LXV): *ACh mutter liebste mutter mein.*

Similarly to the Old Occitan *troubairitz* and Old French women *trouvères*, the vast majority of songs included here reflect more than just a playful strategy to utilize the female voice, since the poets often attack their male lovers quite seriously. As Joan Tasker Grimbert emphasizes: "there is no reason to conclude that women were excluded from composing and performing either in the courts or in the marketplace."[54]

Women's participation in public life and culture as patrons, female scribes, and women artists is apparent and has been thoroughly studied. The geographic distribution of powerful women patrons and female scribes can be addressed here only in passing, though it certainly pertains to the larger topic of women's literature, culture, and the arts. For instance, Ottilia Fenchlerin (ca. 1592), who had commissioned a song-book for her own library, lived in Strasbourg; Clara Hätzerlin copied a songbook in Augsburg on behalf of her patron Jörg Roggenburg in 1471; and the women's songs in the Zürich songbook (ca. 1600) are of South German or Swiss provenance, etc.[55] The same distribution is true

---

[54]   Joan Tasker Grimbert, "Introduction," *Songs of the Women Trouvères*, ed., trans. and introduced by Eglal Doss-Quinby, Joan Tasker Grimbert, Wendy Pfeffer, and Elizabeth Aubrey (New Haven and London: Yale University Press, 2001), 11.

[55]   *The Cultural Patronage of Medieval Women*, ed. June Hall McCash (Athens and London: The University of Georgia Press, 1996); unfortunately, the German-speaking lands are practically ignored here. See, however, Joachim Bumke, *Mäzene im Mittelalter: die Gönner und Auftraggeber der höfischen Literatur in Deutschland 1150–1300* (Munich: Beck, 1979), 231–47; Bumke limits his investigation to the period up to 1300. The

for the religious songs. Most of these were originally published in a nineteenth-century multi-volume anthology edited by Philipp Wackernagel, *Das deutsche Kirchenlied* (1864–1877).[56] In his time he had access to a large number of private collections, many of which today have either been lost or dispersed. His editorial principles were meticulous and reliable, always strictly text-based, which allows us today to use this extraordinary multi-volume anthology in the quest for women's religious songs. The anthology is especially useful because Wackernagel drew on libraries and archives located all over German-speaking lands.

About the translation
All texts contained in this collection were composed in the late fifteenth and sixteenth centuries. Their authors were more concerned to correlate their words with the music, less with the syntactical, rhetorical, logical, and even grammatical precision and correctness of their texts. The religious poems, however, demonstrate a specific background based on a Biblical account, making it considerably easier to translate their early-modern German text into modern English. The secular love songs are much more reflective of personal idiosyncrasies, not only in content, but also in language, irrespective of occasional dialect variants. Moreover, the medium is poetry, that is, verse structures, rhyme schemes and patterns, which privilege sound over meaning. My intentions are always to render the German texts into as precise and correct English as possible while staying as close to the original as possible. This occasionally requires a rearrangement of verse lines, conjectures, additions, and even interpretations. In remarkable cases I have made a note of the difference between the literal and the poetic translation. In cases where I had to add words or even short subordinate clauses to explain the implied meaning, these additions are placed in square brackets. In clear contrast to older strategies in translating medieval and early-modern literature into English, I have made no attempt to recreate the rhyme scheme or the poetic meter. Certainly, this might lower the literary quality, but the reader is invited to consult the original, available in my two editions (*Deutsche Frauenlieder*, 1999; *'Mein Seel fang an zu singen'*, 2002) or

---

contributors to *Deutsche Frauen der Frühen Neuzeit. Dichterinnen, Malerinnen, Mäzeninnen*, ed. Kerstin Merkel and Heide Wunder, 2000, on the other hand, contrary to their own claims, primarily examine seventeenth- and eighteenth-century women authors but not women patrons.

[56] Philipp Wackernagel, ed., *Das deutsche Kirchenlied von der ältesten Zeit bis zu Anfang des XVII. Jahrhunderts*, 5 vols. (Leipzig: Teubner, 1864–1877; rpt. Hildesheim: Georg Olms, 1964).

in any of the older text anthologies, and consider the translation as an aid to understanding these German women's songs in the original. The form of German used by the poets is already considerably removed from classical Middle High German, but it has not yet fully developed into early-modern German as utilized by the Baroque writers. Where the title of a song is the same as the first line of the poem (in which case the historical broadsheet usually did not contain a separate title), the translation is not repeated in the heading to the song. Typically for late-medieval and early-modern German texts, the orthography does not follow strict guidelines, as often is demonstrated by the erratic use of capital letters and other inconsistencies.

Acknowledgments
It is my pleasure to express my thanks to Jane Chance for inviting me to contribute to her series Library of Medieval Women. She had to nudge me for several years but I was not ready until 2002, after my second volume with German women's religious poetry had appeared in print. Anne Winston-Allen (Southern Illinois University, Carbondale) was kind enough to read the Introduction and to provide me with valuable suggestions and comments. I am very thankful to Jean E. Jost (Bradley University, Peoria, IL) for reading the chapter with religious songs and offering her critical input. Kari McBride (University of Arizona, Tucson) read the Interpretive Essay and offered welcome suggestions. My good friend, William C. McDonald (University of Virginia), read a large section of this book, providing valuable corrections. I also want to express my appreciation for the editorial assistance given by my graduate student Kathleen Shull. Thanks are also due to an anonymous reader of Boydell & Brewer. I owe them all my gratitude.

I would like to dedicate this volume to my good friend Jean Godsall-Myers.

Translation

Women's Secular Songs

I. Selection from the *Ambraser Liederbuch*, 1582

The *Ambraser Liederbuch* was copied by an anonymous scribe or scribes for Archduke Ferdinand of Tyrol (1529–95) and contains 262 popular songs of erotic and religious content. Ferdinand placed this book in his personal library, clearly expressing his interest in these kinds of texts. The *Ambraser Liederbuch* was based on the *Frankfurter Liederbuch*, first printed in 1578, and reprinted in 1584 and 1599.

No. 1 (Ambras No. XXXVI): *HErtz einiges lieb, dich nicht betrüb*

1. Heart, my only love, do not be sad,
Although the time right now combats us
You will easily see that every person here on earth,
However happy she ever might live, how elevated she might be,[1]
Will, from time to time, experience some misfortune.

2. Live just like me, this I ask of you,
Just as hope can never fail us,
We will always err, realize this.
What infidelity can do, consider this,
With all my heart I hope you will experience some good.

3. After such sorrow, seek my loyalty,
Which will always be there for you,
And I will always be obliged to you, this is true,
I will never leave you, not even an inch away.

4. With joy all your sorrow will be compensated.
This song appealed to the wise people.
It was composed by a beautiful virgin.

---

[1] The poet uses the masculine pronoun "er" in reference to the masculine noun "mensch" ('person'), but this has no specific meaning with regard to the gender identity of the poet.

No. 2 (Ambras No. LII): *MEin alter man, der nimpt sich an*

1. My old husband has determined
To steal my joy and happiness.
With grumpiness and bickering he causes me pain,
I wish he would give it up.
He bickers with me and mumbles under his breath, checks the entire house;
When he sees that I am joking happily
With a [male] guest, he is deeply troubled
As he experiences great pain [jealousy].

2. He wants me, it often happens,
Never to laugh.
Through his manners he transforms me into an old person,
Since I must shun all joys.
This causes me pain, as I am not used to it,
But I am learning it from him.
He makes me decide to ignore it,
I will simply disregard [his command].

3. What's wrong with him not to let rest,
Day in and day out, his jealousy.
When he is at home, he is searching [for me] outside,
And [particularly] fears the young people
Who go around at night and dare him
With playing the flute, with singing, and courting.
Their loud noise makes him sick
As I can tell by watching him.

4. Dear husband, you cannot take
A joke in your old days,
Though you know quite well that young people
Need entertainment and joy.
Why are you castigating yourself, so that you, like me,
Will not love enough?
Be of good cheer, this will enliven you.
And do not be so gruff and sorrowful.

No. 3 (Ambras No. LXV): *ACh mutter liebste mutter mein*

1. "Dear mother, my dear mother,"
Said a young sweet virgin,
"I cannot live for pure suffering.
Whenever I think of the students,
Their beauty affects my heart,
I have given them my love."

2. The mother said: "Dear daughter,
Do not be disturbed about this,
What can you do with a student?
I want to find a merchant [as a husband] for you,
With whom you can live happily
The students do not have any money."

3. The young woman did not think about it for long
And quickly answered her mother:
"Your words cause me pain,
The merchant must keep away from me,
I want and must have a student,
As I tell you from the bottom of my heart.

4. I do not care about riches or great wealth,
The students please me much more,
No one will turn my mind away
From this honorable fraternity
That is considered with great respect everywhere,
In all countries and all cities.

5. I have never given my love
To those who work in the field of trade or who are alcoholics,
And those who have not learned anything.
[My lover] must be an independent student,
To whom I will entrust my honor,
As he has studied at the university.

6. The students' life pleases me,
As they all enjoy great honor,
They are well educated
And are crowned with many virtues.[2]
No one is more beautiful than they,
This reputation no one can take away from them.

7. Oh, when they walk around
They shine like the morning star.
Who does not feel attracted to them?
Who does not love their playing of the lute
When they strike the strings
And stroll about playing their instruments and singing?

---

[2]   The meaning of this line remains somewhat unclear; literally it seems to say: 'many things
make their appearance look great.'

8. Only the students win the prize,
I am singing only their praise with all my might,
They lead a wonderful life.
It is a joy to be with students,
As they eloquently joke
And express themselves so charmingly and endearingly.

9. Good-bye and good night, you merchant,
[We women] do little care for your pleading,
You do not need to wait for me.
Hail to you with the elegantly feathered hats.[3]
My mind and heart are turned only toward you.
I always long for you."

10. She who sang this little song for us anew,
Is called a goldsmith's daughter.
She has sung this song very well.
She mightily cherishes the students,
Who all are respectable good fellows.
Her singing went very well.[4]

No. 4 (Ambras No. CIX): *ACh Gott wem sol ichs klagen*

1. Dear God, to whom can I reveal my sorrow,
My secret suffering?
My heart is about to despair.
I am made prisoner,
As I have been forced to enter a convent
Already in my young life.
I must live there
With no joy or happiness,
Which I bitterly lament.

2. Now listen to me
Hear what I want to tell you:
Cursed be all my friends
Who have convinced me to join the convent.

---

[3]   The poet might also mean: 'you with the good feather [i.e., quill],' which would refer to the students' activity of writing, and moreover might carry a phallic meaning.

[4]   For the problematic nature of this and similar "women's songs" where, as it seems, a male poet assumes the female voice as a mask to express deeply misogynistic attitudes, see Ann Marie Rasmussen, *Mothers and Daughters in Medieval German Literature* (Syracuse: Syracuse University Press, 1997), 163–88.

How could I have defended myself against that[5]
Against which there is no defense.
My friends consume all my wealth
And heavily burden my soul,
Which I dearly lament to Christ in heaven.

3. I know of another [monastic] order,
And I do not want to stay in this one.
This I have realized fully,
As I have been deceived by people's lies.[6]
These have shackled me tightly
For almost twelve years.
Now I have discovered the truth,
I have been released from my ropes
And I have lost all my piety.

4. The order that I have in mind
God has created Himself,
It is the order of marriage alone
As it has been described in Holy Scriptures.
It is not good for man, God says,
To stay alone,
Therefore He created another person
Out of his flesh and bone,
Another person who provides him with help.

5. These two were Adam and Eve
Whom God has bonded together.
They were charged to obey this order
And not to break their vows.
They were told to earn their bread with sweat
And hard work
Otherwise they would have to die
And be condemned in all eternity,
Probably to hellish pains.

6. Let us follow this ideal,
May God help us in our effort.
May Christ take care of us
Who will protect us all the time.

---

[5] The poet uses the present tense, though the content clearly requires the present perfect tense.
[6] Literally: 'people's fiction.'

Let us trust in him alone
And not in any human person.
He alone can nourish us
And keep us from false teachings.
May He be praised and honored.

No. 5 (Ambras No. CXCII): *SEhnlicher schmertz*

1. Pain of longing
Affects my heart with sickness
And this is no laughing matter.
I woefully lament
That my good fortune
Is about to be slain
Because of his evil tricks,
Which I will tolerate no more.
Whatever I do in my life,
Because of many evil people,
And wherever I turn
My honor as a woman is always endangered.

2. If I experience misfortune
And if things turn out with me the same way[7]
As they developed
For Lucretia,
Who then would want to blame me
For my action?
If I were a new Porcia,
Then it would be just appropriate [for me].
To protect my honor
As did Julia and the pure Dido.[8]

---

[7] Despite the use of the simple past tense in the original, the translation requires the present tense to make sense of the narrative development.

[8] These are references to famous women in classical Roman literature who committed suicide or experienced harsh punishments. Lucretia (ca. 510 BCE) killed herself after she had been raped by Sextus Tarquinius, to clear her name and that of her family for posterity. Porcia (ca. 95–42 BCE), the wife of Brutus who murdered Caesar, committed suicide after her husband's death. Julia (d. 14 CE) was Augustus's daughter and wife of his successor Tiberius in his second and her third marriage; in 2 CE her father had her banished to a remote island as punishment for her many adulteries and public debaucheries. The mythical Dido, queen of Carthage, killed herself after she had been abandoned by the Trojan Aeneas whom the Gods had ordered to found Rome. See *Women's Roles in Ancient Civilizations. A Reference Guide*, ed. Bella Vivante (Westport, CT, and London: Greenwood Press, 1999).

3. But I truly hope
To see the day
When womanly virtue[9]
Will be rescued, as it happened to Susanna.[10]
Because of her innocence
And great patience
And God's mercy
The two old [judges] experienced suffering and woe.
Therefore I hope
That the time will come [as He will realize]
And it will be just fitting
That God will not have forgotten me.

II. Selection from the *Heidelberger Liederhandschrift*

This voluminous manuscript was first discovered by the Romantic poet
and journalist Joseph Görres in 1817. It comprises 179 pages with 205
songs, probably written down by two scribes. All songs were originally
composed prior to 1550, which we can confirm with the help of other
songbooks written at a later date and which contain copies of songs bor-
rowed from the Heidelberg manuscript. Not much further information
about this songbook is available.

Heidelberg No. 83: *Ach Gott, ich klag dir meine nott*

1. Oh God, I lament about my misery to you:
I am so badly hurt that I almost die
And I have given up [all my hopes]
I thought I had chosen a dear lover,
But now he has abandoned me.

2. He loved me, he cherished me,
I did whatever his heart desired
In virtue and with honor—
[Now] he loves another [woman] much more than me,
He has left me behind, left me behind.

3. What good will your false trickery do to you, lad,
As you are so disloyal!

---

[9] Literally: 'beauty of women.'
[10] Her tragic account is contained in the Old Testament, Dan. 13; see Albrecht Classen, "The
   Emergence of Modern Drama out of Late-Medieval Shrovetide Plays. The Case of 'Das
   Leben der heyligen Frawen Susanna'," *Medieval Perspectives* XIV (1999): 35–49.

You need no longer wait for me!
I have known of your betrayal for a long time,
Which hurt my heart, my mind, and senses.

4. If I had known of your disloyalty before,
I would not have desired your love,
You have lied so often,
Go away, go away . . .
You are expelled from my heart, yes, from my heart.

5. She who sits on a thistle tree[11]
And trusts young lads
Is unfortunately blinded:
You men are always true to your kind,
Weeds do not disappear from the garden.

6. Once I had an apple—it was delightful and red,
It has hurt me fatally,
There was a worm inside;
Forget about this red apple,
I must pluck it from my mind.

III. Selection from the *Liederbuch der Ottilia Fenchlerin*, 1592

Little is known about Ottilia Fenchlerin and why she commissioned the
scribe Caspar Schröder to produce a songbook, completed on May 22,
1592, for her. She lived in Strasbourg, as Schröder himself states in the
prologue to this songbook, but his dedication remains very brief and does
not reveal any other biographical details: "all these extraordinary songs are
written down in this book in honor of Ottilia." Originally the manuscript
was housed in the Fürstlich Fürstenbergische Hofbibliothek in
Donaueschingen, but it was sold to the Badische Landesbibliothek in
Karlsruhe in 1994 (Cod. Don. 121). This songbook contains a surprisingly
large number of women's songs, perhaps because of Ottilia Fenchlerin's
interest in women's erotic poetry. There is practically no scholarship avail-
able on this songbook, and no traces of Ottilia Fenchlerin's name are left
in the Strasbourg archives, as my own inquiries have confirmed.[12] Imagery,

---

[11]   Although the poet uses the masculine demonstrative pronoun "der," the subsequent line
makes it fully clear that this pronoun refers to a woman.

[12]   The translation is based on the edition by A. Birlinger, "Strassburgisches Liederbuch,"
Alemannia 1 (1875): 1–59; for some early, though not very illuminating comments, see
Arthur Kopp, "Die Straßburger Liederhandschrift," *Alemannia* 44 (1917): 65–93; for a

style, content, thematic issues, and linguistic features provide relatively solid evidence for the authentication of previously unknown women authors. Considering the frankness with which these poets reveal their emotions—if these are not simply poetic projections—it is not surprising that their texts have come down to us anonymously.

No. 1 (Ottilia No. III): *Freündliches herz*

1. Friendly heart
       Your love has embraced me
   Without causing any pain,
   Yet because of you I suffer,
   My desire is directed at you
           Fed by true desire,
           Believe me that,
   Inspired by deep love.
           As long as I live
           [I beg you] do not turn away from me.
   You are my help, my consolation here on earth.

2. Friendly image
       Display your grace
   Toward your poor woman servant,
   When you want to, it can disappear,
   Take me into your arms
           Filled with joy
           Snuggled to your chest,
   You arms hold me tightly.
           As long as I live
           Please never abandon me.
   My desire always goes out toward you.

3. My friend and treasure
       Hear my words,
   Take them to heart,
   I fear that I have lost my love,
   For which I suffer great pain.
           Do not turn away from me,
           I'll give you a gift,
   You will hear me singing

critical reading, see Albrecht Classen, "*Ach Gott, wem soll ichs klagen.* Women's Erotic Poetry in Sixteenth-Century German Songbooks," *Neuphilologische Mitteilungen* XCVIII, 3 (1997): 293–318.

Well considered
At a proper time at night:
You are my darling paramour
I hope it will turn out well for me.

No. 2 (Ottilia No. VIII): *Ich bin schabab, macht mich nicht graw*

I have lost my lover, but that won't turn me grey,
I hope my case will turn out well!
Good luck,
Whatever the result is,
Keep yourself well and take care:
Your repeated cheating
Proves to be my good fortune,
Just as he wishes,
I do not ask for very much
In return for his jealousy,
However our relationship might develop,
I will learn through my loss,
Who knows how long this tragedy will hurt me.

2. He said to me: "be gone,
I don't want your advice,[13]
Who asks for it?
I am in no hurry."
I know what hour the clock has struck:
It is obvious
That he no longer loves me,
Me, poor maid,
I am totally rejected,
And when I beg him [for his love]
He does not grant my wish
He won't fulfill it,
Since he shies away from doing so[14]
Even if I ask him for it once again.

No. 3 (Ottilia No. XV): *O trauren über trauren*

Oh sorrow above all sorrow,
How can I feel happiness

---

[13] Literally, the first two lines seem to express just the opposite, as he says: 'be my guest, / I will consider your advice in future.' The context forces us, however, to read the somewhat cryptic lines as negative statements.

[14] Literally: 'as he shies away from this ride.'

As I have lost
My most beloved paramour.
And yet I do not want to lament this loss
Instead I want to be happy.
I know a beautiful young man
Who is as attractive to me as the other one was.

2. He has broken off our relationship,
[But] I hope this will be my good fortune,
He had intended to lead me astray
Using a fool's rope.
I tell you truly:
He will certainly find a richer woman,
Whereas I stem from poor parents.

No. 4 (Ottilia No. XX): *Kein lieberer auf erdt war nie geboren*

1. No one was ever born here on earth
Whom I loved more and whom I liked better,
God Himself had selected him for me,
And I selected him myself
Among all beautiful young men,
This he must believe me.
I love his noble face,
And he gives so much comfort,
By God, I wished I were with him.

2. In that case my pain would be gone,
And gone would be my laments,
I hope to find
The one my heart desires!
I found him in the roses.
It is my heart's desire,
To break many of the little flowers
So that I can caress him
If only he would understand my words.[15]

3. "Good-bye my dear, good night
May God keep you well."
She did not think for long about it

---

[15] For clarity's sake lines 5–10 had to be rearranged in the translation. The poet tends to switch tenses, which I have tried to unify according to the logical development of thoughts. The last line represents a linguistic problem as the original would translate verbatim as 'If only he would dissolve my speech,' or 'If only he would stop my words by kisses.'

And kissed him on his lips,[16]
When I must leave him
My heart will feel much pain,
If I cannot gain your love,
I will die from [emotional] suffering,
Though I will not feel [physical] pain.

No. 5 (Ottilia No. XXIII): *Gross lust hab ich zu singen gehabt*

1. I had great interest in singing
So I wrote this little song.
I sing it for you so that you may be
My most beloved and remain that way!
I sing this song for an attractive young man,
I hope he will not be hostile to me,
Oh God, send my greetings to this young man.

2. His noble comportment pleases me well,
He acts just as a young man should,
He has two brilliantly shining eyes
And attractively curly hair.
He struts like a true nobleman,
He has [beautiful] red lips,[17]
Oh God, send my greetings to this young man.

3. Oh you sweet lover, do not forget me
And keep me in your mind,
I would always like to be with you.
Whatever you want me to do, allow me to do.
Oh, if everything went right for me
Your mother would have to be my mother-in-law,
Oh God, send my greetings to this young man.

4. I wished that God would let me experience that year [in which we
    marry]!
All that I wish for you, may it come true,
Yes, if it were not to become reality
By God, I would be buried!
I wished, fine young man, I would be yours
And you would be mine.
Oh God, send my greetings to this young man.

---

[16]   It is surprising that the poet here suddenly resorts to the third person singular, whereas the
    rest of the stanza is in the first person singular.
[17]   Literally: 'little red mouth.'

5. I am a wild little doe,
I am hunted by a beautiful delightful image.[18]
I cannot find pleasant enough words;
I would like to be beautiful, but I am not.
I am certainly pious, but it does not avail,
Therefore I do not have a steady paramour!
I am truly a wild little doe,
I am hunted by a beautiful delightful image
When I try to catch him by appealing to his honor
He always jumps away from my [hunting] ropes.
I will sing a lovely song for you, you beautiful one.

6. Good-bye, dear beloved, I am departing,
I hope you will soon answer me
Which will please me,
So that no evil-minded courtly spy will deflect me[19]
From the one man who is not mentioned and yet well-known,
From him who is of high birth and excellent,
I hope my love [for him] will not be lost.

7. Fine young man: I have composed this little song for you,
I send you many thousand good-night wishes;
When I composed this little song
I thought of you very often,
You are a jewel in my heart,
If you are drawn to me, please let me know,
Send me greetings, it is now your turn.

No. 6 (Ottilia No. XXV): *Mein freüdt wiewol sie verloschen ist*

1. Though my joy has been destroyed,
I still hope at this moment
That it will return to me
As you will never, my beautiful lover,
Disappear from my heart.

2. All my hope I entrust to you,
Hold on, most beloved friend,
To true love and loyalty,

---

[18] Literally: 'beautiful, forest-happy image.'
[19] There is no appropriate term for *Klaffer* in English, nor in modern German either. It could mean a rival in love, or a spy hired by the parents or a husband. It could also simply mean a jealous or envious person, or a member of the household who reports the singer's secrets to the authorities. The expression *Klaffer* disappeared in seventeenth-century German literature.

. . . . [20]
You will never regret it.

3. Pure sweet young man, keep in mind
Not to give away your heart and loyalty to someone else,
You are the only one in my life,
You are my love, help, and consolation in every misery,
I cannot resist you.

4. [But] I am forced to stay far away from you, dear beloved,
Which causes my heart heavy pain,
It cannot feel any happiness,
As long as I am deprived
From my highest consolation here on earth.

5. Oh beloved, consider this great pain,
That now affects me so badly,
That I cannot see you at all,
Which causes me heavy pain,
That fills my heart with sorrow.

6. All joy and happiness are gone,
I am, truly, very sad all the time,
Because of what I have lost,
My only consolation in this world,
How can I recover it?

7. My heart is filled with true love
And I think of you by day and night,
Your beauty has captured me
As I am ensnared by burning love,
I feel a strong desire for you.

8. In suffering I will stand by you,
Even if it is hard for me,
My dear young lad,
I am ready to accept death for you:
If only I might be successful!

9. You are the only one who gives me happiness
And drives away my sorrow,
If I could see you again
And if you could be with me and I with you,
Nothing more wonderful could happen to me.

---

[20]   Here some lines are lost.

10. I know that everything will first be demolished
Before my heart will let go of you,
I have no regard for anything here on earth,
You alone are my joy and happiness,
You should be mine [in marriage].

11. Do not tear the twine of love[21]
(Which connects you with me),
Be steadfast in eternal loyalty,
Otherwise you will rip open my wounds.
Take my heart with you,
Otherwise I will never regain my health.

12. I always place my heart
In your hand, beautiful young lad,
And all my confidence:
Hold me tight, as I hold on to you,
Allow me to build [my trust] solidly on you.

13. To Christ, who gives us blessedness,
I entrust you, my heart's beloved,
He will certainly protect you,
He will give you consolation
He is full of goodness.

14. Do not move away from me, I beg you,
always stand by me like a rock!
Uphold your loyalty
which you have promised to me:
then no one will be able to separate us.

15. She who composed this little song for us,
Is called a tender young maid,
Strong love has filled her heart,
A fine young lad loved her
With whom she could not unite.

No. 7 (Ottilia No. XXVIII): *Feins lieb ich muss dich meyden*

1. Dear beloved, I have to stay away from you:
This is all the fault of courtly gossipers!
My secret love for you causes me much pain,
[But don't worry] beloved heart, I can wait for you,

---

[21] Literally: 'cloth of love.'

My heart is caught
In the prison of love for you,
My desire goes toward you,
You are the one I love alone.

2. My heart is saddened
And mortally wounded,
Your love affects me painfully,
your red lips are the cause of it.
I look forward to the time
When I will be able to see you, my beloved,
As a cold love is fired up again
When you talk to me with loving words.

3. Dear beloved, I won't let you free,
As long as you will live,
Follow your road and street,
Wherever you have a business:
I belong to you,
I am your servant,
I love you more than anybody else,
You are the crown of my heart.

4. Dear beloved, be loyal to me,
As you have promised to me,
You will not regret it.
I say this without malice:
I give myself to you as a gift,
Believe me, this is certain,
I love you more than anyone else
Among all the other young men.

5. Dear beloved, this I sing for you
For a thousand nights,
I cannot come to you,
This is fully clear to me,
Oh separation above all separation,
It turns my joy to sadness.

No. 8 (Ottilia No. XXX): *Vor zeyten was ich lieb vnd werdt*

1. A while ago I was loved and cherished,
Now everything has become sour,
Everything is lost for me
As he wants to love someone else,

No one can serve two lords [at the same time]:
One has to love the one
And give up the other,
That is my own experience.

2. Listen, you dear maids,
Take care of yourselves
So that you won't be forced by love
To pay for it dearly.
Being easy allows you only to realize a short goal.
Do not believe the young fellows too much,
Today's love will be tomorrow's pain
As a result of men's lack of constancy.

3. They know how to play with the falcon
While we are together with them,
They know how to use many proverbs
Whenever they leave us,
They promise much and do not keep anything.
We must be their prisoners
While they hold us tight with a fool's rope
For the rest of our lives.

4. They lure us and sing deceptively,
Until we fly to them.
This way they fool us,
While we fly around restlessly,
Just as one does with the little birds in the woods,
The hunters whistle sweetly and lure them,
And when they are caught,
The hunters kill them with a club.

5. I say good-bye for a thousand nights
My sorrow has been put aside.
Had I realized your disloyalty long ago,
My heart would have turned away from you.
Truly, I would have let you feel sorrow,
But now you can deceive another woman than me:
Your disloyalty teaches me that soon I won't care about you anymore,
Be well in this good night.

No. 9 (Ottilia No. XLII): *Ach Gott ich thu dich bitten*

1. Oh God, I beg you
Give me reason and understanding

In these bad times
So that I might be able
To withstand this evil, vicious world
Which is full of evil deception,
For I will tell you
What happened to me.

2. A young wild man
Made me truly happy,
With his red lips,
He has seduced me,
He said many alluring words to me
Until he had overpowered me
And made it impossible for me to stay where I once was,
This he managed to do.

3. He promised me his love,
But with false intentions:
My heart was about to break
When I could no longer visit him,
Which happened because he feigned love for me
that he falsely claimed to feel.
He is repenting now
That he ever tried it with me.

4. He said with clever words,
That he loved me most,
He would not turn away from me
As long as I would live.
He promised me this
Swearing with his tender right hand,
That our love would be constant and strong
And would never change.

5. When I gave him credence,
When I believed his words and promise,
I said to him tender things
Which I do not want to reveal here,
Oh dear, what great misery
I had to suffer afterwards:
As he abruptly turned from me
And led me by the fool's rope.

6. That gave me much suffering
Much lament and great pain.
There was no joy in my heart,

I wished death came to me:
His love had embraced me,
Truly I am in love with him,
I am filled with more longing for him
Than for silver and shining gold.

7. Take note, all you young maids,
Watch out for the tricks of the young men!
Do not let love impose torture on you,
As it is very bitter.
Its beginning might well be sweet,
But keep the end in mind,
When lovers must part from each other,
Then follow lament and sorrow.

No. 10 (Ottilia No. XLIII): *Auss argem wahn*

1. Filled with serious suspicion
Do I begin
To lament about a young man,
I sigh and cry
That in all my life
I have not lost any sweeter person
I lament about this loss very much
And the more time passes the more I do.
That I can no longer see you
Causes me heavy sorrow:
Love of my heart, this I lament to you,
I beg you for your help.

2. Help me, love of my heart
To get out of such suffering!
Give me, love of my heart
Your loyal advice.
Much is falling upon me
For which I am not prepared,
Nothing comes my way
That I desire.
I am miserable
And totally worthless,
And if things do not change soon,
I will have to die because of extreme suffering.

3. Listen to my words,
You fine paramour,

While I must shun you:
Lament with me, sun and moon,
Lament with me, leaves and grass,
Lament with me, everything that is covered by the sky,
Lament with me, beautiful horses,
Lament with me, little birds,
Lament with me, little flowers on the meadow,
Lament with me, joyful earth,[22]
Oh God in heaven,
You know how painful the separation is for me.

No. 11 (Ottilia No. XLVIII): *Ein freündtlichs aug zu mir wenken*

1. Turn a friendly eye toward me,
Fulfill my heart's desire,
I think of the beloved,
Oh God, if only he were with me,
Is this not a wonderful life,
Heart, mind, and all my senses
Go for the most beautiful one whom I have selected
Mighty God, let me be with him,
I love him more and more as time passes.

2. How heavy is my suffering!
When I am not with him
I feel like a prisoner in chains,
When he has fettered my heart,
Is this not a wonderful life,
[Listen,] heart, mind, and all my senses,
Deep down at the bottom of my heart,
I say it to myself over and over again,
Oh, how could I be happier!

3. No one can give me consolation,
When I am so deeply filled with sadness,
As no one else but my most heart-loved man
Is always on my mind.
He is the one whom I think about.
My heart, mind, and senses
And the love that I feel for him
Will not be detected by any spy,
I will let it be known only to my beloved.

---

[22]   Literally: 'happy brown thing.'

4. What should I worry about the spies' tongues,
When they do not hurt me or you,
Since we had to separate,
I have only thought of you,
Wherever you might be traveling around in the world,[23]
I will always wait for you;
Likewise, do the same for me
As I do for you, my beloved.

IV. Selection from Clara Hätzlerin's Songbook

Many more medieval women worked as independent scribes than we
would normally assume. Literary production was not simply an exclu-
sively male domain: many women enjoyed a higher educational level
than their male contemporaries, at least in the world of the courts.
Medieval convents, including women's convents, were always centers
of education and higher learning. The cultural situation in late-medieval
cities was very complex because of the different schooling systems and
women's heavy involvement in their husbands' businesses (craftsman-
ship, health care, trade, etc.), which made it necessary for them to
acquire at least some basic education.

Here I am concerned with one outstanding urban scribe, Clara
Hätzlerin, who is known for her professional activities in Augsburg in
the late fifteenth century. As a professional scribe she produced several
important public documents, such as the *Schwabenspiegel* (a major South
German law book), books dealing with the crowning of Emperor Frederick
III (1467) and with falconry (1471), and a major city law book. Clara
Hätzlerin was also commissioned by a member of the Augsburg elite, Jörg
Roggenburg, to create a *Liederbuch* (songbook), which she completed in
1471.[24] Clara's songbook contains a remarkable selection of the best

---

23 Literally, 'wherever you might ride over the meadows' or 'over the open fields.'
24 *Liederbuch der Clara Hätzlerin*, based on a Manuscript in the Bohemian Museum in
Prague, trans. and with an introduction and glossary by Carl Halthaus, Bibliothek der
gesammten deutschen National-Literatur, 8 (Quedlinburg and Leipzig: Gottfr. Basse,
1840; rpt. with an epilogue by Hanns Fischer, Berlin: de Gruyter, 1966); see also Burghart
Wachinger, "Liebe und Literatur im spätmittelalterlichen Schwaben und Franken: Zur
Augsburger Sammelhandschrift der Clara Hätzlerin," *Deutsche Vierteljahrsschrift für
Literaturwissenschaft und Geistesgeschichte* 56, 3 (1982): 386–406; Johannes Rettelbach,
"Lied und Liederbuch im spätmittelalterlichen Augsburg," *Literarisches Leben in Augsburg
während des 15. Jahrhunderts*, ed. Johannes Janota and Werner Williams-Krapp, Studia
Augustana, 7 (Tübingen: Niemeyer, 1995), 281–307; Sheila Edmunds, "Clara's Patron:
The Identity of Jörg Roggenburg," *Beiträge zur Geschichte der Deutschen Sprache und
Literatur* 119, 2 (1997): 261–67.

fourteenth- and fifteenth-century German lyric poetry, such as songs by
Heinrich der Teichner, Peter Suchenwirt, Suchensinn, Muscatblüt, Oswald
of Wolkenstein, the Monk of Salzburg, and Hans Rosenplüt. Clara also
included a number of anonymous songs that strongly imply female author-
ship and were primarily addressed to a female audience. The scribe obvi-
ously chose poetic texts that represented the most popular songs of her
time, from which we may deduce that women's personal concerns
expressed in verse also appealed to the general public.

No. 1 (Hätzlerin No. 104): *Ich went, ich hett mir vszerwelt*

1. I thought I had chosen [to my delight]
A young man whom I could fully trust;
But then he put me in the second row,
Thanks to another woman
Who has pushed me aside as his most favorite
Using a deceptive strategy.
I hope to be able to get my revenge,
There is no doubt about it.

2. He broke the promise he gave me,
This causes me much pain and joy!
I hope I will get my revenge
So that I can hurt him badly.
I hope someone will cheat on him
Just as he has on me.
He turned away from me
And left me behind in false hope.

3. His love service truly lies in shambles,
He deceived me for a whole year.
He did it deliberately to me,
As I can see clearly.
Nothing else gives me any worry,
Since I cannot change it.
I am only concerned about being publicly ridiculed
And being mocked for my lost love.

4. Alas, alas, I have been betrayed,
The degree to which I am hurt
Gives pleasure to this young man,
Whenever he thinks of it.
Nevertheless I wish him all the best,
As I cannot suppress [my love for him].

But now I will let him go,
However long it might take.

5. So long, I have received my freedom,
Though I hardly wanted it,
As he has put on brown clothes[25]
And turned around my boat.[26]
I will let him fly away
with his [miserable] owl companion.
If he thinks that an owl is the best,
I want to have a falcon [instead].[27]

No. 2 (Hätzlerin No. 109): *Praun, plaw vnd weisz*

1. In honor of me
He deliberately wore brown, blue, and white colors
To have me constantly on his mind.
He has, however, abandoned this habit.
Now he is in the service [of another woman]
And wears different colors,
In brown, white, and green
For another beautiful woman.

2. What would happen if,
As a result of my great unhappiness,[28]
I would constantly experience sorrow?
If then I wanted to date again
I would have to destroy this [true] love
Without any lament

[25] The image of 'brown clothes' might imply that he has disappeared in the crowd.
[26] The imagery used here remains somewhat obscure, though the overall meaning is clear: he is no longer in love with her.
[27] The singer specifically refers to the classical topos of the lover as a falcon, developed by the time of The Kürenberger in his love songs (*Des Minnesangs Frühling*, ca. 1160/1170); Helmut Teervoren, "Eber, ber, valke: Kleine wortgeographische Beobachtungen zur Kürenberg- Überlieferung und Deutungsversuche zu Kürenbergs Strophe *Jô stuont ich nehtint spâte*," *Entstehung und Typen mittelalterlicher Lyrikhandschriften*, ed. Anton Schwob, András Vizkelety, and Andrea Hofmeister-Winter, Jahrbuch für Internationale Germanistik: Reihe A: Kongressberichte, 52 (Bern: Peter Lang, 2001), 291–301; Ingrid Bennewitz-Behr, "Von Falken, Trappen und Blaufüssen: Kein ornithologischer Beitrag zur Tradition des mittelhochdeutschen Falkenliedes beim Mönch von Salzburg und Heinrich von Mügeln," *Spectrum Medii Aevi: Essays in Early German Literature in Honor of George Fenwick Jones*, ed. William C. McDonald, Göppinger Arbeiten zur Germanistik, 362 (Göppingen: Kümmerle, 1983), 1–20.
[28] Literally: 'because of the advice of unhappiness.'

Deep in my heart
And eliminate the memory of him.[29]

3. May good luck help me
To do so
Without great effort!
Very soon I will succeed
In winning another lover.
He will woo me
In passionate love!
Him I will favor strongly.

4. I am not so old
To forgo
The bloom of all happiness.
A well of perfect loyalty
Quells up in me.
I want to give my loyal love
Without any hesitation
To another man
And present him with honest happiness.

5. Sorrow, be gone,
Happiness will replace it!
My heart, as I hope,
I will give to another man
Who is more deserving.
He is a man
Who can protect me from sorrow.
All my sadness, go away on vacation!
Thanks to the new love!

V. Selections taken from the *Züricher Liederbuch* and the *Berner Liederbuch*

Many, if not most, late-medieval songbooks were the result of a systematic collection of previously published (manuscript or printed) songs (see the *Liederbuch* by Clara Hätzlerin), although the role of oral transmission should not be discarded entirely. In the case of the *Darnfelder Liederbuch* we know that the owner, Kathryna of Bronchorst und Batenborch, began her collection in 1546 using an empty book, which she had received from

---

[29] The poet uses a complex set of idiomatic images to express the end of her love, which cannot easily be translated. She says verbatim: 'I must pull this thing / without any lament / over my own back, / and escape his memory.'

her parents as a gift, like a poetry album. She copied down some songs herself, and then asked friends, relatives, lovers, later her own husband to do the same.[30] Some songbooks, however, represent a simple assemblage of previously printed broadsheets, perhaps the result of a librarian's or a song-enthusiast's efforts, such as the *Berner Liederbuch*[31] and the *Züricher Liederbuch*.[32] In those cases the term "Buch" or 'book' might not be fully applicable, as the binder simply put together a bunch of individually printed songs (broadsheets) to preserve them for the future.[33] Often each song was introduced with an illustration, sometimes there was a reference to the melody to be used, but very rarely the actual music. The *Züricher Liederbuch* is difficult to date, but according to many of the individual broadsheets included here it might have been produced around 1605–1610. The name of the collector and the history of this songbook remain unknown. This literary document is interesting for us especially because it contains several noteworthy women's songs. The same applies to the *Berner Liederbuch*, though there we find only one woman's song.

As the broadsheets mostly served as a medium to preserve the words only, each stanza is written almost like a prose text, except that the end of each verse is indicated by a '/' (virgula), which also substitutes for the modern punctuation. To convey to the reader what the actual broadsheets looked like in the *Züricher Liederbuch*, I am following the form of the printed text in the present translation of these songs, but in the case of the one song found in the *Berner Liederbuch* I re-establish the traditional verse structure.

Züricher Liederbuch

No. 1 (Zürich No. 50): *Ich hab mir außerkohren* (first printed in Basel in 1605 by Johan Schröter)

1. I have chosen for myself a beautiful and elegant young man / born from a good parent tree / He will be my most beloved / He will find my heart

---

[30]   *Die Darnfelder Liederhandschrift 1546–1565*, based on initial work by Arthur Hübner und Ada-Elise Beckmann, ed. Rolf Wilhelm Brednich, Schriften der Volkskundlichen Kommission für Westfalen, 23 (Münster: Aschendorff, 1976). This songbook also contains a number of women's songs: see my *Deutsche Frauenlieder*, 111–30.

[31]   Today housed in the Stadt- und Bürgerbibliothek Bern, Rar. 63.

[32]   Today housed in the Stadtbibliothek Zürich, formerly under the signature KK 1552, Nr. 50, now under the signature Ms Z VI 686 (in the "Handschriften-Abteilung").

[33]   A very good example, now available in facsimile, is *Jörg Dürnhofers Liederbuch (um 1515)*. *Faksimile des Liedruck-Sammelbandes Inc. 1446a der Universitätsbibliothek Erlangen*, with epilogue and commentary by Frieder Schanze, Fortuna Vitrea, 11 (Tübingen: Niemeyer, 1993).

ready / for good love and trust / no service will be too hard for me / which I will carry out for him.

2. I have often looked at him / and repeatedly sighed deeply / I snuggled up to him / asking him whether he loved me the most / I had sworn an oath / that I loved him truly and completely / as he had chosen me [as his beloved] / but he led me at a fool's rope.

3. Hidden in my heart, I harbored [many feelings] / for so many days / this now causes me severe pains / though I never complain about it to anyone / I have been secretly his mistress / for a long time / I wished he would be the same for me / then my efforts would not have been in vain.

4. I have promised to be loyal / to this attractive young man / may God send me a messenger / so that I can maintain my loyalty to him pure and clean / with all my love and loyalty / my heart is turned toward him / no service will be too much for me / which I will do for him.

5. Let go / let go / I am much too poor for him / in Summer it is easy to hike / when the sun shines so warmly / I have been pushed away from him / I have lost my good fortune with him / I have been attached to a fool's rope for too long.

6. But I do not yet want to despair / to despair / to despair is no good / no one will ever cheat on me [again] / this will help me in the long run / No bird in the air / is like any other / and if he will not become my lover / there won't be a reason for me to commit suicide.[34]

7. He is always in my heart / I never lose him out of my mind / he causes me many pains / when I think of him / I think of his letter / which he had sent to me / I will hold on to it / as long as I will live.

8. Who is the person who sang this song to us / who has sung this song anew / this was done by a good maid / late one evening / she has often sung this song / with a fresh and free mind / she has learned to understand / what the loss of love means.

No. 2 (Zürich No. 53): *DAs ir mich thut verschmähen* (printed in 1616 [no place, no printer])

1. I do not care much / that you reject me / the same thing can happen to you / you are not superhuman / so listen to what I want to tell you / the penalty will follow quickly / as it happened to Narcissus.

---

[34] Literally: 'no need for me to die.'

2. He despised / Echo, the tender maid / which broke her heart / therefore she ran away / and escaped beyond the mountain and through the valley / thus she became an echo / which you still hear often today.

3. Narcissus had to suffer / heavy pains afterwards / because he arrogantly / despised the maid / As a consequence he saw his own figure / [mirrored] in a cold well / and loved it passionately.

4. He [often] looked / deep into the clear well / he hoped to enjoy the sight of the figure / which consisted of nothing but water / and so the beautiful boy / could not give up his love / until he passed away.

5. Was he not, indeed, payed back / with the same currency / while he had despised / the maid altogether / he brought so much misery upon her / that God quickly punished him / and put an end to his life.

6. Therefore I, poor young woman / plead with you, do not ignore me so much / if [only] you constantly strive for nothing / but an aristocratic [amorous] lifestyle / I will be content / as long as I will have been his beloved / and continue to be his mistress.

7. Whoever is filled with arrogance / and contempts his own people [friends/family] / will get himself into danger / so everybody should pay attention / and heed this warning / given by the fall of Narcissus / which was brought about by Echo's echo.

8. You often show yourself / in your most friendly figure / but your heart is like iron / and your love has turned cold / you talk in a friendly manner / but your words do not come from the bottom of your heart / so never forget what I told you.

9. That you destroy me now / young man in your proud mind / will have consequences / as you will realize soon / go ahead without delay / I will find someone more to my liking / patience will overcome everything.

10. God will certainly help me / as I hope / to get revenge on this arrogant young man / who despised me / because I seem to be of too low class and not worthy / for a while I was just right for him / but now he despises me.

11. Since he despises me / I remove him from my mind / even if my heart will suffer badly / just like the fast Echo / I will put up resistance / helped by Cupid / before I have to succumb to death.

12. Oh young saddened heart / let go of such love / do not feel such great pain / which Lady Venus quickly hands out / with bow and arrow / wherever she finds two people[35] / she inflames them immediately.

---

[35]   The text says verbatim: 'wherever she finds two lovers.'

13. Even though I will be quickly rejected / by the young man / I will nevertheless observe moderation / so that I, an honest child, / do not despise and contempt [him] too much / instead consider / his honor and virtue.[36]

14. Above all I must praise / your exceeding beauty / and have to make my best effort in this case / Oh noble consolation for my heart / there is no one here on earth / who displays his worthiness / as this honorable young man does / in virtues and manners.

15. My heart longs for you / by day and by night / while I shed many tears[37] / I have composed this song / I wish you many happy hours / your rose-colored lips[38] / give me joy down to the bottom of my heart.

16. How many pains afflicted my heart / when I saw, filled with pain / my noble treasure[39] / he did not say a word [to me] / turned his eyes away / this [pain] cuts deep into my heart / Oh, woe is me, what pain!

17. He has turned away from me / I suffer it patiently / he crudely insults me / although I do not bear any fault / Oh Lady Jealousy, you are an evil herb / the person who relies and builds on you / does not trust anyone else.

18. Herewith I want to come to an end / Oh young man, shining with virtues / do not be cross with me / keep this little song in mind / I have composed it in a hurry / because you have rejected me / I wish you all [my audience] a good night.

Berner Liederbuch

No. 40/2: *ACh Gott wem soll ichs klagen*[40]

1. Oh God, to whom shall I address my lament?
My heart's beloved has turned away from me.
I am about to despair.
Misfortune is waiting outside of my door,
My only consolation is

---

[36]   This stanza requires considerable rearrangement of the lines and some additions to allow an English reader to understand it.

[37]   The poet uses two alternative terms for 'tears', "Zähern vnnd Threnen," but the meaning is the same.

[38]   As so often in this late-medieval love poetry, the lover's gaze goes toward the lips, but the image used here is, verbatim, 'the rose-colored mouth.'

[39]   The meaning is 'her noble lover.'

[40]   To demonstrate the contrast, I will rearrange this poem according to its verse structure, although the printer also utilized the continuous line with virgulas serving in place of commas and periods.

That the situation is everywhere the same
As fortune will return,
I am not the first [and only] one [to suffer from this pain].

2. There is no one here on earth
Whom I loved more in my life
I hope he will become my lover
He who gives joy to my heart
In his attractive appearance,
He called me his bride-to-be,
But the wind has turned
Now I am separated from him.

3. Blessed and blissful was my life
The hour when my heart
Recognized in him
The one I love the most.
Then my heart was wounded
Which I hardly survived.
When I still could embrace him
My heart became fresh and healthy again.

4. I have experienced through him
Many sorrows and pains
As I am filled with suffering
To the bottom of my heart,
Oh, the woeful time
Filled with constant sadness,
I will not find any consolation
When he parts from me.

5. He regularly called me
His only and most beloved treasure,
He also let me understand
That he could not live without me,
He never would turn away from me,
But now I have been abandoned,[41]
I have lost his favor,
Although it is not my fault.[42]

---

[41] The word "schabab" is one of the key terms in late-medieval German love poetry, express-
ing the woman's experience of having been dumped, betrayed, or deceived by her lover.

[42] Because of the exigencies of the song structure, at times the wording in these love songs
proves to be very restricted, occasionally requiring to read the opposite meaning into the
text. This could be the case here as well, as it makes little sense to translate verbatim: 'as
it is my own fault.'

6. Yet I do not want to cry,
I have to leave him quickly,
I stay true to my words and deeds[43]
Although now the wind
Is turning back and forth
And tosses me around so much
That I have to mourn all the time
And will never regain my happiness.

7. My heart could break
When I think of the time
When he [still] talked to me,
No one gave him more happiness [he said]
Than I, his consolation, all alone,
He wanted me to be his beloved,[44]
This now hurts my heart,
My misfortune is great.

8. I could despair out of sorrow
Right now at this time.
Who will help me bear this suffering
Which has fallen into my lap
Together with fear and sadness?
Oh what miserable times!
I have enough reasons to cry
About what lies in my heart.

9. No tongue can repeat
The sweetest words
Which often were secretly
Exchanged between us
[But] fully honorable
And which gave me so much joy.
Now everything has turned topsy-turvy
And transformed into suffering and sorrow.

10. If my saintly life
Does not affect his heart
Which wants to give up on me completely
And throws me away in an act of mockery
Then his heart must be harder
Than all rocks and stones.

---

[43] Literally: 'I mean it truly.'
[44] Literally: 'to be his own.'

Now I turn away from him,
There must be an end to this.

11. With very saddened heart
Do I often sit alone
Burdened with sorrow and pains
Here in my bedroom.
When I think about him
I almost faint.
May God change it all to the better,
This I beg him to do in my lamentations.

12. Hope always offered me the advice
Not to give up on him
Only until now, as I have learned through my loss
And have painfully experienced it.
His completely disloyal mind
Constantly turns back and forth.
No man will ever cheat on me again
As long as I will live.

13. Oh, is there hope for this sad life?
Who has ever invented you?
I have to give up on my love,
As you have thrown me into sorrow
And into great misery.
I lament about this to my God,
Much rather would I suffer
The bitter, sour death.

14. At least one more time at last
I want to beg him from the bottom of my heart
To gracefully consider
All my [intense] pains
And accept me again in his grace,
Which I have lost without any fault [on my part],
And give me his love anew;
I am waiting that he will do this.

15. All my hope . . . (text loss)
. . . is mixed (text loss)
I place . . . (text loss)
He knows the right time limit.
Just like the cool dew
Provides refreshment in the green meadow
To the herbs [and plants] for ever and ever,
So I have given it to my lover.

16. His attractiveness has inspired me
To compose this song,
At the end (or: for his teaching) I have sung it
Based on a sad story,
I have composed it only for him alone
Although he probably
Will look down upon it.
I have sung it exclusively for him
For 1000 good-night occasions.

VI. Selection from humanist songbooks

Traditionally, literary scholarship has tended to make a clear distinction between the late Middle Ages on the one hand and, on the other, the Renaissance and Humanism with their reorientation toward classical learning, a more open world-view (*curiositas*), and a modern university education, leading to the adoption of modern ways of thinking about human life, social conditions, religious orientation, and the world beyond the European continent. However, this demarcation does not apply quite so well to popular song poetry, particularly in the vernacular. A number of significant sixteenth-century German songbooks were compiled by humanists such as the Nuremberg scholar Hartman Schedel, Johannes Heer, minister in the Reformed Church in Glarus, Switzerland, the Nuremberg medical doctor Georg Forster, and the Basel humanist Ludwig Iselin—but the interest in popular poetry proved to be quite traditional. The songbooks of Forster and Iselin include some women's songs, but we do not know whether Schedel or Heer recognized them as such or whether they incorporated them into their collections for some other purposes.

Johannes Heer of Glarus[45]

Johannes Heer (b. ca. 1489 in Glarus) studied at the University of Paris (Sorbonne) from 1508 and graduated with a Master's degree (*Magister artium*) in 1510. Soon afterwards he came into contact with the famous Zürich minister Ulrich Zwingli. He continued with advanced studies in theology, completing them in 1516. Subsequently he served under Zwingli as his chaplain. However, Heer did not fully convert to the

---

[45] *Das Liederbuch des Johannes Heer von Glarus. Ein Musikheft aus der Zeit des Humanismus (Codex 462 der Stiftsbibliothek St. Gallen)*, ed. Arnold Geering and Hans Trümpy, Schweizerische Musikdenkmäler, 5 (Basel: Bärenreiter, 1967).

Reformed Church until 1529. He died around 1553. By 1510 someone had given him as a gift the volume in which he copied down the popular songs. In that year Heer entered most of the secular songs (nos. 1–58); only afterwards did he also include religious songs.[46]

No. 1 (Heer No. 4): *Ach, hulf mich leid und sendlich klag!*
(Melody composed by Adam of Fulda)[47]

1. Oh, help me in my suffering and lamenting! Never during my life
Have I enjoyed any rest. My heart, in a hurry,
Wrestles with pain
It struggles and throbs
Because of past happiness.
Although I am worried that my love[48] that I feel for him
Is all lost, I can in no way
Ignore him or hate him
Either out of love or grief.
I, poor maid, have always been inspired
With much hope. Nevertheless,
He betrayed
This new love
That grows from a noble heart. I have never felt
So miserable. Whether I go, stay,
Sleep or wake: I am afraid
That I lack in patience,
What can I do
To get children?[49]
His gracefulness will be my loss
And pain, what a joke!
Heart's beloved friend,
Come back. Nothing I desire more
But to embrace you, hold you
To my breast, as it was previously my great joy.

---

[46] Beat A. Föllmi, "Heer, Johannes," *Musik in Geschichte und Gegenwart*, 2nd completely rev. ed. by Ludwig Finscher, Personenteil, vol. 8 (Kassel, Basel, et al.: Bärenreiter, Metzler, 2002), 1144–45.

[47] As is often the case in late-medieval love poetry, an old melody composed by Adam von Fulda (ca. 1445–1505) was used for a new song—a strategy called *contrafactum*. The emphasis of this song rests on the melody by itself, whereas the text does not always make full sense. For Adam von Fulda, see http://www.bautz.de/bbkl/a/adam_v_f.shtml

[48] Verbatim: 'favor.'

[49] Literally: 'to acquire heirs.' The meaning of this line remains obscure, especially as the poet seems to have cared more for the internal rhyme than for a reasonable development of the song's plot, unless we accept my conjecture that the female singer indeed expresses her hope to get pregnant soon.

This song is also included in **Ludwig Iselin**'s songbook of 1574–75 (see below),[50] but there it is followed by a second stanza (No. 51):

2. My sorrowful request should inspire you.
Although I am not very beautiful, your attractiveness is not
Any better than mine: it fades
In light of my art.
Physical beauty comes to an end with some pain
Quickly followed by joy and strength.[51]
Then loyalty turns into repentance,
Lost in the fire of this love.

[the following lines 35–39, here left out, are incomprehensible and do not contribute to the development of the song's content]

Dear friend, quickly consider this,
Turn your heartfelt desire
Toward me and say: I
Am yours; my blood
Boils, it wants to free you from your pain,
Let go of your laments, do not ask any further,
That is my request from you, my highest treasure,
Your words charm
My senses, now I burn every day full of laments
Beyond all measure,
Truly, I will never let you go.

3. You will observe that I will not disregard
Any of your service, none of your quests will leave me cold .
You are the one who can increase
Ladies' honor.
I, the miserable maid, ask you for one thing,
I do not request anything else: allow me
To fully enjoy
The fruit of love.[52]
If you grant this to me, I will feel more happy than ever before
In my whole life,
While I struggled and fought[53]
To win my love.

---

[50] Today housed in the University Library of Basel, FX 21, Musikhss.; text quoted from Max
     Meier, *Das Liederbuch Ludwig Iselins* (Basel: Werner-Riehm, 1913).
[51] Literally: 'courage.'
[52] Verbatim: 'to go on the pasture of love.'
[53] The poet uses many verbs to express the same thing, probably to meet the musical exigencies.

I have never been caught in illusions.
Neither writing nor any other activity,
Neither crying nor lamenting
Helped me at all
To avoid and fend off this misery.
Beloved, turn around, come quickly running [to me] and hurry,
While I am still alive,
Otherwise no [medical] art will help
To sustain me without your presence,
As I clearly notice,
My heart wishes you to gain full honor.

No. 2 (Heer No. 21): *Ach Gott, wie wee tuot scheiden*[54]

1. [Woman] "Good Lord, how painful is the separation!
My heart is seriously wounded
And causes me woes and suffering
And sorrow all the time.
My joy and high spirit have abandoned me,
My heart is wounded,
When will I [ever] regain my happiness?"

2. [Man] "I felt in my mind
Just as if I were with her.
She is an empress,
And I do not desire any other lovely woman.
She lies so heavy in my heart
I must laugh for pure joy
Whenever I think of her."

3. [Woman] "If you intend to ignore me
As many a man does,
Please rather take my life.
So far I still possess a free mind.
Heart's beloved, do not despair,
As long as I am living
I will give you many thanks."

4. She who has sung to us
This new song
Was a young maid.

---

[54]   This song consists of a man's and a woman's stanzas, but the last lines still indicate female
authorship. We might call this poem a "Wechsel" or 'Exchange.'

She sang it in a lovely night
It deals of her lover who was beautiful and fine.
I wish her all the virtues
Now the song must come to an end.

Ludwig Iselin

Ludwig Iselin was born in Basel on July 2, 1559 as the son of Professor
Ulrich Iselin and Faustina Amerbach. His father died in 1564, and
Ludwig was raised by his uncle Basilius Amerbach. In 1574 Ludwig
entered the University of Basel, and from 1581 he also studied at the uni-
versities of Geneva, Bourges, and Padua, before returning home. In 1589
he received his doctorate in law from the University of Basel where he
began to teach. Twice, in 1597 and 1607, he was appointed President of
the university. Ludwig was married to Anna Ryhiner and they had six
children. When the Black Death, or plague, killed five of them, he fell
into deep depression and died at the early age of thirty-five on December
2, 1612. Ludwig's friend and fellow student Georg Hug had given him
the songbook as a gift when he went to the university in 1574. Ludwig
added a number of songs (Nos. 48, 50, 55, 56, 61, 64, 68, 69, 70, 78, 79,
80, 81, 83, 97, 115, and 116) and completed the collection by the end of
the following year. On the basis of the content of the earliest songs we
can conclude that the songbook was begun in 1525. Today it is housed
in the Universitätsbibliothek Basel (FX 21, music manuscripts).[55]

Iselin No. 109: *Ich armes maidlin klag mich seer*

1. I poor maid have much to lament,
What will happen with me,
Now that I have not seen
My most-beloved for a long time,
Who entertains me so well,
There is no one to compare him with.
When I think of how he is doing,
My heart is filled with sadness.
My lover must come back to me.[56]

2. Oh mighty God, give me luck,
Wherever he might be in the world,

---

[55] Max Meier, *Das Liederbuch Ludwig Iselins*, 5–9.
[56] Literally: 'the most beloved must be mine.'

Protect his beautiful body
From danger and also from dishonor!
I will be thankful all my life, oh God,
In the day, in the night, and at every hour.
I am looking forward to your return,
You are my only consolation, my most-beloved friend,
Do not forget me who stays loyal to you.

3. He did not depart voluntarily,
He still holds my heart in his possession,
I entrust all my fortune to him.
I will show him all my favor.
He never could detect any falsity in me
In any of my behavior.
This young man is so cheerful,
I would never take any emperor's gold instead of him,
My beloved must be mine.

4. He traveled away, to my chagrin,
He who was the choice of my heart,
He is decked in my colors
When he travels far away.
His separation [from me] causes me much pain,
So I am very much looking forward to his return.

You who are my only consolation, you, my beloved spouse,[57]
Do not forget me in your heart.

VII. Selection from the *Bergliederbüchlein*

Many of the miners who worked in the mining industry of the fifteenth and sixteenth centuries participated in the composition of popular songs. Surprisingly, in one of the volumes of miners' songs we find several women's songs.[58] The term 'miners' songbook,' however, does not necessarily imply that all composers were miners. More realistically, these songs were collected by and for miners in an area where the mining industry was very strong. In fact, most of the songs have not much, if anything, to do with mining.

---

[57] The term "elib" literally translates as: 'spousal love.'
[58] *Bergliederbüchlein.* Historisch-kritische Ausgabe, ed. Elizabeth Mincoff-Marriage, together with Gerhard Heilfurth, Bibliothek des literarischen Vereins in Stuttgart, CCLXXXV (Leipzig: Hiersemann, 1936); Wolfram Steude [Kurt Gudewil], "Bergreihen," *Die Musik in Geschichte und Gegenwart,* 2nd completely rev. ed. by Ludwig Finscher, Sachteil, vol. 1 (Kassel, Basel, et al.: Bärenreiter, Metzler, 1994), 1413–17.

No. 1 (*Bergliederbüchlein* No. 11): *Du falscher Hertzens-Dieb*

1. You deceptive thief of hearts,
Cupid, you mischievous boy,
Go away with your love
And leave me alone,
You have, unfortunately, hit me well,
Alas, how blind I am
To hope that I could
Run after you,
Oh, you poor child.

2. If I had followed the one
Who honestly told me:
Go away before I'll get into trouble,
Oh, if I had chased him away,
I would not have been hurt,
My honor still would be pure.
Now it is already torn,
People intend, people intend
To hurt your integrity.[59]

3. It is indeed true,
I do not lie to you,
My tummy is heavy like a lump,[60]
I have to walk outside of the gate,[61]
The court sergeants are looking for me,
Now I have to avoid the city,
Have to avoid, have to avoid,
Everyone abandons me.

4. When I think of the time
When I was still a virgin,
When I, filled with highest joy,
Bound up my hair,[62]
When I ran to the dance parties
Both in the morning and in the evening,
Afterwards I got, as a result from the dancing,

---

[59]   Literally: 'people run, people run, / around one's legs.'
[60]   She is pregnant.
[61]   Meaning, she is ostracized for carrying an illegitimate child.
[62]   Traditionally this was a clear signal that she was still a virgin: see Kim M. Phillips, "Maidenhood as the Perfect Age of Woman's Life," *Young Medieval Women*, ed. Katherine J. Lewis, Noël James Menuge and Kim M. Phillips (New York: St. Martin's Press, 1999), 1–24, here 8.

A big belly, because of the dancing,
A child in my body.

5. What am I to do
With my full tummy,
As I cannot walk?
This is a new custom.
I must drown myself,
Oh, if only I had a rope
I would hang myself right here,
Hang myself, hang myself,
And would disappear from this world.

6. Oh dear little child,
What shall I do with you?
You lie there swathed.
Oh God, what a horror!
Who will give us nourishment?
Who will preserve our life?
I must sell everything;
I must run to the merchant;
The godfather also must give something.

7. Oh, you cursed love,
How did you mislead me,
You are worse than a thief,
When you made my tummy swell,
Now you laugh at me
Because I have a young prince.
My heart is breaking,
Go ahead and laugh, laugh,
It is just a gift from God.

No. 2 (*Bergliederbüchlein* No. 22): *Was soll ich nun beginnen*

1. What am I to do now
In this dark night?
Oh dear, I poor maid,
I have been woken up from sleep.

2. My mother's hens
They have a rooster
Who makes love to them all
As often as he can.

3. When other maids
Stand at the corner with their paramours,
I poor girl
Have to go to bed alone.

4. When others lie in bed
And enjoy rest and peace,
I poor girl lie there
And cannot close one eye.

5. When others make love with each other[63]
In all their joyous life,
Then I, poor girl, lie [alone]
And lament my loneliness.

6. Oh happiness, oh happiness,
You are a miraculous thing,
I am concerned about the sheath,
And others about the blade.[64]

7. If I have to wait much longer,
I will be in bad shape,
Oh dear me, I poor girl,
I am not getting a man.[65]

No. 3 (*Bergliederbüchlein* No. 23): *Vater, laß dichs doch erbarmen*

1. Oh father, have pity on me
And let me have a husband
Who takes me into his arms
And gives me a warm cover
Who holds me tight to his chest
And gives me a kiss of love.
I detest the life of a virgin,
Come and help me out of my misery,
Come and ease my pain,
I no longer want to be a virgin.

---

[63] Literally: 'When others are engaged in fighting.'
[64] Clearly a pornographic allusion to the vagina and the penis.
[65] Here, more than in all other songs, we might suspect that the poet is male and uses the female voice for dramatic, especially erotic purposes.

2. I strongly desire for the marriage hood[66]
Like the tom-cat lusts for the cat,
Like the male pigeon lusts for the female pigeon,
In just that way I am looking for my treasure,
Even if he might have lost half a leg,
He still would be my lover.

3. Even if he were to use crutches,
Walked in shoes without soles,
I would obediently accept him
And provide him with a warm bed.[67]
What do I care about the world
As long as I like him.

4. I swear by the great jug
Which stands there near the milk jar
That I will win a man
Before year's end,
I have my mind set on it,
I am not made for the convent.

5. Away with you, nuns, away with you convents
You only want to have virgins,
I prefer a man who can give love to virgins,[68]
I prefer him over the money in the convent.
I rather eat a poor diet in the convent.[69]
I am determined to enter marriage.

VIII. Selection from miscellany manuscripts

Much of late-medieval literature has been preserved in miscellany manu-
scripts which often contain an amazing kaleidoscope of texts representing
a wide variety of text genres and subject matter. Sometimes one can
detect a certain order, or arrangement of texts, especially if the collector,
book binder, scribe, or printer intended to group together certain related
documents, such as sermons, didactic narratives, travelogues, literary

---

[66] The "haube" was only worn by married women, serving as a metaphor in the proverbial
saying 'unter die Haube kommen,' to get under the hood, or to get married: see Lutz
Röhrich, *Das große Lexikon der sprichwörtlichen Redensarten*, 3 vols. (Freiburg, Basel,
and Vienna: Herder, 1992), vol. 2, 674–75.

[67] Literally: 'give him a warm cover.'

[68] Literally, 'consoler of virgins.'

[69] The original says: 'convent meat I do not like.'

narratives, cooking instructions, legal documents, Shrovetide plays, love poems, or religious songs.[70] In one of these manuscripts—today Münchener Staatsbibliothek, Cgm 439—from the late fifteenth century, we also find a remarkable woman's song.[71]

No. 3: *Die maid preist ihren getreuen* (The maid praises her loyal lover)

Most joyfully I have become the girlfriend
Of a man whom I have chosen
Among all people.
Surely he loves only me
More than anybody else here on earth.   5
His heart is subject to his desire
Both with honor and respectability.
My heart is also ready for him all the time.
Therefore my mind is deeply grieved
That I cannot be with him every moment.   10
Oh God, if I could see him without any interruption
I would not feel any sadness.
I would receive so much happiness from him
That I would consider everything in life to be like the sound of a violin.
He is my death, he is my life,   15
I have handed myself over to him
In trust and honor
And trust that no one will threaten
His absolute lordship over my heart.
He certainly loves me without any deception.   20
If I were to hear something different about him
That would hurt me and my honor.
Then I would rather die,[72]
As I would not want to pursue
False love with him[73]   25
And would never see him again.
Yet I have never heard from him anything else

---

[70] Sarah Westphal, *Textual Poetics of German Manuscripts, 1300–1500*, Studies in German
      Literature, Linguistics, and Culture (Columbus, SC: Camden House, 1993).
[71] Here copied from: Adelbert von Keller, ed., *Fastnachtspiele aus dem Fünfzehnten
      Jahrhundert*, 3rd Part, Bibliothek des Literarischen Vereins in Stuttgart, XXX (Darmstadt:
      Wissenschaftliche Buchgesellschaft, 1965; rpt. of the 1853 edition), 1404–06; see also Tilo
      Brandis, *Mittelhochdeutsche, mittelniederdeutsche und mittelniederländische Minnereden.
      Verzeichnis der Handschriften und Drucke*, Münchener Texte und Untersuchungen zur
      deutschen Literatur des Mittelalters, 25 (Munich: Beck, 1968), 53–54. As in all other cases,
      a copy is included in my volume *Deutsche Frauenlieder*, 155–56.
[72] Verbatim: 'rather he should have given me death.'
[73] Literally: 'as I would not have wanted to be affected by false suffering.'

But that he feels love for me.
He would never ask a favor from me
Which he wanted me to comply with   30
Were it to harm my honor.
When I think about him intensively,
My love for him grows all the time
As long as I live, by my honor.
I have surely never won more happiness in love   35
Here on earth under the sun.
Whoever would want to alienate him from me,
Would want to take away all my joy.
If there were anything I would like to ask from God
And which he would truly give me,   40
I would ask him to let me stay with my lover.
This, alas, cannot be,
Which causes great trouble for my heart,
And I experience great pain.
When I have to avoid him, this means my death.   45
To be separated from the lover, filled with longing,[74]
Is worse than to be hanged.
Whatever I have heard about the [painful] separation of lovers,
Still my heart's pains are certainly greater.
Alas, alas, and ever alas!   50
Separation means that I will never be able to laugh freely,
Separation is a bitter herb
Which robs me of my heart's lover.
Secretly I suffer from my love for him
As a result of my separation from him.   55
A moment seems like a long year.
Oh separation, you make me so sick,
And I have no bigger lament
Than that I am separated from you.
Although there is no alternative,   60
Yet my heart badly longs
For his love and his presence[75]
And pines away with every fiber.
Whatever I might do
Is dominated by my longing.   65
Longing for him might destroy me,
Patient waiting is my best bet.[76]
I am completely obsessed by my longing.

---

[74]   For rhyme's sake, the poet used the verb "belangen" instead of "sehnen" as the verb in the
       following verse is "erhangen."
[75]   To create a rhyming couplet, the poet used the word 'gut' (= property) for 'body.'
[76]   Literally: 'best inheritance' ("pest erben").

I never forget him for a moment,
when I sleep or am awake, or when I do something,   70
Longing steadily creeps into my heart.
Longing often makes me sick,
Longing gives me much boredom,
But if I did not have a glimmer of hope,
I would never gain a moment of rest.   75
[Indeed] Hope takes away much heaviness [from my mind].
If there were no hope,
My heart would long have perished.
And I would not have been set free.[77]
When I think [of him] and am filled with good hope   80
I am always in a happy mood
And demonstrate openly through my behavior
That I see myself bonded with him,
Because it might easily happen
That a sick person can get well through a happy heart,   85
As I am currently happy
And consult many times with my heart
And think back and forth
Weighing many plans
How I could get to him.   90
If I could hear his words directly
My heart would be rich with joy,
This I hope every day
And I wish him all the best.
May God bestow upon him a constant mind   95
In proper love and loyalty.
May God give him luck and blissfulness,
May God preserve his health,
May God let him have much joy,
May God not allow that he will fail in his well-being,   100
May God protect him from all evil things,
May God protect him at all places
And especially from the false words by the spies.
If I were certain about all this,
My heart would suffer less pain   105
And I would have no reason to lament.
May God give him a constant mind every day.
I have never learned anything more important:
The person who wants to preserve constancy
Must stay constant [himself or herself] without any fickleness.   110
I cannot think of anything better

---

[77]   Syntactically the sentence would have to be translated as: 'and would hope not have set me
free,' but to avoid the repetition of the noun required the rearrangement into a main clause.

Since constancy is a great virtue.
The person who, already in her youth,
Strives for constancy all the time
Will experience great joy   115
As constancy provides the heart with strength.
It is advisable to be good friends with a constant person
Because much joy should grow in us.
One needs to fight failing constancy.
Everybody should reflect upon this   120
And should consider it and strive
To develop constancy
And marry a constant woman.
Then this person will undoubtedly acquire
Everything he desires with her heart.   125

IX. Georg Forster's songbooks

One of the most important collectors of late-medieval songs was the Nuremberg medical doctor Georg Forster who edited five volumes of popular poetry between 1539 and 1556. Whereas the earlier volumes enjoyed considerable success on the book market and had to be republished several times, the later volumes seem to have exerted less appeal. This might well reflect a general decline of interest in these types of songs during the second half of the sixteenth century, at least in Nuremberg where humanism and public debates about the Protestant Reformation weighed heavily on the minds of the audience. Moreover, the poetry by the Mastersingers (*Meistersinger*), such as Hans Sachs—that is, poetry composed by members of the guilds—mostly replaced classical courtly love poetry and, in its wake, other traditional, especially popular song poetry. Nevertheless, some of the poems copied down by Forster were used by leading contemporary composers such as Orlando di Lasso (ca. 1532–94) and Leonhard Lechner (ca. 1553–1606) as text bases for their songs.[78] Here we also find some women's songs.[79]

---

[78]   Georg Forster, *Frische Teutsche Liedlein (1539–1556)*, Part One: *Ein Auszug guter alter und neuer teutscher Liedlein (1539)*, ed. Kurt Gudewill, text revision by Wilhelm Heiske, Das Erbe deutscher Musik. Erste Reihe: Reichsdenkmale, 20. Mehrstimmiges Lied, 3 (Wolfenbüttel and Berlin: Georg Kallmeyer, 1942). This Georg Forster is not to be confused with the German writer Georg Forster (1754–94) who accompanied Captain Cook on his second journey around the world and became a famous natural scientist, travel writer, and philosopher.

[79]   Rebecca Wagner Oettinger, "Forster, *Vorster*, Georg," *Musik in Geschichte und Gegenwart*, 2nd newly rev. ed. by Ludwig Finscher, Personenteil, vol. 6 (Kassel, Basel, et al.: Bärenreiter,

No. 1 (Forster I, No. 67): *Viel Freud nährt mich zu aller Stund*

1. Much joy sustains me at all times.
He who grants me this is an honorable person.
I will give him my red lips [for a kiss].
Often I recover my health when he desires me.
So I do, so I do what behooves me
And what does not lead to my seduction here on earth?
There is no one who will see me in a different light.

2. Oh H., you, more than anyone in the world, grant me your love!
It does not matter to me
If anyone is opposed to it.
I have pledged my loyalty to him.
The way how he treats me
Without any falsity
Pleases me mightily
And do nothing but what I really should do.
My heart is filled with love for him.[80]

3. With him I have full hope
That he will be a loyal lover
And will not deviate from this ideal.
My mind and feeling have no other orientation
Than toward him.
That is all I desire,
He is the right one, and that is true
Even if I lived hundred thousand years,
No one will enjoy more love and loyalty than he.

No. 2 (Forster I, No. 178): *Mein hertz hat sich mit Lieb
verpflicht't zu dir*

1. My heart is committed to love you,
So the fabrications by the spy will not distract me
Even if he might die[81]
Because of his false hate and evil envy
Or his poisonous hatred.

Metzler, 2001), 1501–05; see also my study "Georg Forsters Liederbücher im 16. Jahrhunderts: Letzte Blüte und Ausklang einer Epoche. Rezeptionsgeschichtliche Untersuchungen zur Gattung des spätmittelalterlichen Liedes," *Lied und populäre Kultur. Jahrbuch des Deutschen Volksliedarchivs* (forthcoming [2004]).

[80]   Literally: 'My heart is filled with my will toward him.'
[81]   Literally: 'even if his neck will break.' This refers to the evil spy.

Do not think that for these reasons I would avoid you!
I do not pay attention to any disapproval,
Whether it is reasonable or not.[82]

2. I love you in every respect
Entirely according to my wishes and ideals.
I receive endless joy
From you, especially
Since you have no shortcomings.
False rumors are really mean,[83]
Therefore the spy's strategy
Does not achieve its desired end
Since everybody knows who he is.

3. All that good fortune that I wish and grant him
Goes toward the gossip-monger.
His disloyalty cannot remain
Unrewarded,
As will become apparent in no time.
As loud as he might speak up
I do not give a dime for his blabber,
He is missing the target by far.
My heart is in love with you [my man].[84]

No. 3 (Forster III, No. 8): *Hertz liebster man*

This song would have to be read as a complementary composition to III, No.
7 (here not translated), in which a bridegroom addresses his future wife,
whereas in No. 8 it is her turn to remind her husband of her expectations of
him:[85]

1. Heart's beloved man,
Whatever might be your desire
Will also be my desire.

---

[82] The last two lines are formulated in a very tight manner, forcing some interpretation.
Literally they read: 'I do not tolerate any disapproval, / even if it were the most reason-
able.'

[83] The German word "Mist" means 'manure' and is still used in contemporary German to
express general disagreement or dismay over a certain unfortunate situation, like modern
English 'damn' or 'shucks.' The term is used in a very casual manner and is not supposed
to break any taboo.

[84] The entire stanza has to be read as a drastic satire against those who are jealous of her love.

[85] For the topic of affective marital love poetry and other types of texts in the history of early
modern German literature, see Alfred Weber, *Affektive Liebe als rechte eheliche Liebe in
der ehedidaktischen Literatur der frühen Neuzeit* (Frankfurt a.M.: Peter Lang, 2001).

I promise you loyalty
And will live with you
According to your wishes
And as you desire.
I will make my best efforts,
So help me God
Who will protect us from suffering.

2. [Dear husband], avoid evil company
Stay away from them,
Do not desire
What does not belong to you,
Whatever does not burn you,
Do not think of touching it.
Avoid evil gossip,
Do not undermine someone's honor.
Be smart and quiet,
Do not give in to gossiping,
That is my desire.

3. May your lifestyle
Be free of any blemish,
May the morality of your bed
Be protected.
Preserve your honor
Do not go to parties all over the place.
Stay at home.
Go out into public [only] with me,
Unless it is necessary,
If you want to behave according to my wishes
Then follow these rules.

X. Selection from Wolfgang Strizer's songbook, 1588

Nothing is currently known about this particular songbook, and schol-
arship has never made any effort to critically examine this collection.[86]
This is, unfortunately, rather typical for the entire genre as many song-
books have either never been studied and continue to languish in the

---

[86] *Neue Teutsche Lieder mit vier Stimmen, mehrertheils ad pares voces componirt Durch
Wolffgangum Striccium Saxonem, ersamen Landschafft in Crain Cantorem* (Nuremberg:
Katharina Gerlachin, 1588), here quoted from Karl Goedeke and Julius Tittmann, *Liederbuch
aus dem sechzehnten Jahrhundert,* Deutsche Dichter des sechzehnten Jahrhunderts, 1
(Leipzig: Brockhaus, 1867), no. 23.

archives or have been ignored for a long time after they had been reprinted in the nineteenth and twentieth centuries.[87]

No. 23: *Für allen, die da sind geboren*

1. Among all those who have been born
I have chosen you, beautiful beloved,
Whoever wants to is free to hate this,
You are the joy of my young heart
And you soothe all my woes and pains.

2. My heart is joyous and cheerful
And experiences happy times,
Whenever I can be with you.
But when I have to leave you,
My heart feels sorrow and pain.

3. I am constantly filled with burning desire
For the happiest of all times,
I long to see you again
And want to sit on your lap,
While looking at your red lips.

4. I do not care a bit
That there are so many jealous people
They only try to make me feel bad.[88]
One beggar begrudges another,
If he sees him standing in front of a door [and having success with begging].

5. If you love me as I love you,
And do not love any other woman aside from me,
I do not have any other wish,
Then I would know without any doubt
That your heart is honest and pure.

6. She who sang [composed] this song for us
Did not experience any boredom with her lover,

87 Albrecht Classen, *Deutsche Liederbücher*, 2001, 89ff., 195ff., 245ff., 307ff.; for an example of how to make these songbooks available again for modern research, see the facsimile of *Jörg Dürnhofers Liederbuch* (ca. 1515) by Frieder Schanze, 1993; for the reception history of these songbooks far into the seventeenth century, see Rolf Caspari, *Liedtradition im Stilwandel um 1600. Das Nachleben des deutschen Tenorliedes in den gedruckten Liedersammlungen von Le Maistre (1566) bis Schein (1626)*, Schriften zur Musik, 13 (Munich: Musikverlag Katzbichler, 1971).
88 Literally: 'it is nothing but mockery.'

She did not have too much time on her hands with him
She enjoyed her love with him.
In such a case the heart has the time of its life.

XI. Selection from Jacob Regnarts's and Leonard Lechner's songbook, 1579[89]

This songbook is known to us only through a secondary source which identifies the composers of the melodies, Jacob Regnarts and Leonard Lechner, but we do not know the names of the poets. The following song, however, is clearly identifiable as a woman's song.

Nach meiner lieb viel hundert knaben trachten

1. Hundreds of young men are vying for my love,
But the only one whom I love does not care about me,
Oh dear, I poor maid, I will pass away because of my sorrow.

2. Every [man] desires to be my paramour,
The one alone whom I love destroys me,
Oh dear, I poor maid, what can I do about it?

3. Everyone else promises me many good things,
The one alone whom I love does not want to see me.
Oh dear, I poor maid, what will happen to me?

4. None among all those men can resist my attraction,
The one alone whom I love does not want to succumb,
Oh dear, I poor maid, what good does my life then do?

---

[89]   Originally composed by the noble and famous Jacob Regnart musician at the Imperial court for three voices in the fashion of the Italian *Villanelle* reedited by Leonard Lechner Athesinus *Newe Teutsche Lieder*, Erstlich durch den Fürnemen vnd Berhümbten Jacobum Regnart, Röm. key. Mai. Musicum, Componirt mit drey stimmen, nach art der Welschen Villanellen. Jetzund aber . . . Durch Leonardum Lechnerum Athesinum . . . (Nuremberg: Katharina Gerlachin und Johanns vom Berg Erben, 1579); here quoted from: Karl Goedeke and Julius Tittmann, *Liederbuch aus dem sechzehnten Jahrhundert*, 61, no. 60.

Women's Religious Songs

Introduction

Whereas in the case of secular women's songs one can only guess whether the internal references provide enough justification to identify the texts as compositions by female poets, this information is usually much clearer in the case of religious songs. In many church songbooks, and in a large number of private song collections used for personal meditation, fifteenth- but mostly sixteenth-century women poets made their voices heard, demonstrating that literary and artistic creativity was not an exclusively male domain. Until recently, however, the map of late-medieval and early-modern German literature was deplorably marked by blank spots because hardly any German women writers from that period were known to us, if we disregard the famous Argula of Grumbach and Anna Ovena Hoyer.[1] New research, however, has yielded a surprisingly large number of noteworthy women writers. To some extent the Protestant Reformation was a major factor in creating some free space, particularly for aristocratic and urban women, but we do know of some contemporary Catholic women poets who composed church songs.[2] Whereas in the Middle Ages monastic convents provided an important framework for women to write poetry and compose liturgical music, which was then closed to a large extent in Protestant areas during the early sixteenth century,[3] early-modern women of both denominations found a new avenue for their self-expression through the genre of the church song. This, however, does not necessarily mean that women's composition was restricted to church song, since we may assume that women probably also composed other types of fictional text.[4]

---

[1] Albrecht Classen, "Die 'Querelle des femmes' im 16. Jahrhundert im Kontext des theologischen Gelehrtenstreits. Die literarischen Beiträge von Argula von Grumbach und Anna Ovena Hoyers," *Wirkendes Wort* 50, 2 (2000): 189–213.

[2] Elisabeth Schneider-Böklen, *Der Herr hat Großes mit mir getan. Frauen im Gesangbuch*, 2nd ed. (Stuttgart: Quell, 1997; orig. 1995); though written for the lay audience, this book was one of the first to explore Protestant church song with respect to women's contributions.

[3] See, for example, Jeffrey F. Hamburger, *Nuns as Artists. The Visual Culture of a Medieval Convent* (Berkeley, Los Angeles, and London: University of California Press, 1997). See also Wendy Slatkin, *Women Artists in History. From Antiquity to the 20th Century* (Englewood Cliffs, NJ: Prentice-Hall, 1985).

[4] See the contributions to *Deutsche Literatur von Frauen*, Vol. 1: *Vom Mittelalter bis zum Ende des 18. Jahrhunderts*, ed. Gisela Brinker-Gabler (Munich: Beck, 1988).

Although the sixteenth century was deeply influenced by the monumental struggle of the Protestant Reformers against the Catholic Church, first leading to the Protestant Reformation and later to the Catholic Counter Reformation,[5] a vast number of readers/listeners were nevertheless still interested in purely secular themes, as is clearly documented by the so-called *Volksbücher* (chap books) or prose novels, the many *Liederbücher* with their large quantity of *Volkslieder* (popular songs), and dramas.[6] At the present time, however, it is very difficult to determine whether any one of those fictional, especially non-religious, texts was indeed composed by a woman. Fortunately, this situation is beginning to change since it has been possible to locate a considerable number of (anonymous) women's songs where a female voice at least claims authorship (see above).[7] Moreover, women's actual contributions to the Protestant Reformation have been thoroughly studied in the last few years, leading to many surprising discoveries.[8] To gain solid ground for our

5   Herbert Walz, *Deutsche Literatur der Reformationszeit. Eine Einführung*, Einführungen (Darmstadt: Wissenschaftliche Buchgesellschaft, 1988), provides a good overview of the literary history of the sixteenth century and also discusses some of the women writers from that time. See also Roland Herbert Bainton, *Women of the Reformation in Germany and Italy* (Minneapolis: Augsburg Publishing House, 1971).

6   Albrecht Classen, *The German Volksbuch. A Critical History of a Late-Medieval Genre*, Studies in German Language and Literature, 15 (Lewiston, NY: Edwin Mellen Press, 1995; rpt. 2000); Classen, *Deutsche Liederbücher des 15. und 16. Jahrhunderts*, Studien zur Volksliedforschung, 18: Volksliedstudien, 1 (Münster, New York, Munich, and Berlin: Waxmann, 2001); Wolfgang Suppan, *Deutsches Liedleben zwischen Renaissance und Barock. Die Schichtung des deutschen Liedgutes in der zweiten Hälfte des 16. Jahrhunderts*, Mainzer Studien zur Musikwissenschaft, 4 (Tutzing: H. Schneider, 1973).

7   See also the various contribution to *Medieval Woman's Song. Cross-Cultural Approaches*, ed. Anne L. Klinck and Ann Marie Rasmussen, The Middle Ages Series (Philadelphia: University of Pennsylvania Press, 2002). The problem with almost all references to alleged women's songs in this anthology rests with the deliberately postmodern blurring of the distinction between a true woman's song and a female voice and the attempt to define "the type by textual rather than authorial femininity" (2). Certainly, "[f]ocusing on textual femininity avoids the biographical fallacy on the one hand, and, on the other, the nihilism which concludes that in a system dominated by men there can be no such thing as a woman's voice . . . " (2). But if it no longer matters whether a text was actually composed by a male or a female poet, the whole "feminist" argument becomes essentialist again by default. The argument for medieval women's poetry is much better grounded in *Songs of the Women Trouvères*, ed., trans., and introduced by Eglal Doss-Quinby, Joan Tasker Grimbert, Wendy Pfeffer, and Elizabeth Aubrey (New Haven and London: Yale University Press, 2001), 1–44.

8   Albrecht Classen, "Frauen in der deutschen Reformation: Neufunde von Texten und Autorinnen sowie deren Neubewertung," *Die Frau in der Renaissance*, ed. Paul Gerhard Schmidt, Wolfenbütteler Abhandlungen zur Renaissanceforschung, 14 (Wiesbaden: Harrassowitz, 1994), 179–201; *Convents Confront the Reformation: Catholic and Protestant Nuns in Germany*, introduced and ed. by Merry Wiesner-Hanks, trans. by Joan Skocir and Merry Wiesner-Hanks, Women of the Reformation, 1 (Milwaukee: Marquette University Press, 1996); Peter Matheson, "Breaking the Silence: Women, Censorship, and the Reformation," *Sixteenth Century Journal: Journal of Early Modern Studies* 27, 1 (1996): 97–109; Martha W. Driver, "Women Printers and the Page, 1477–1541," *Gutenberg-Jahrbuch*

further investigations, we are now in a position to identify women's actual contributions at least in the field of religious poetry. What inferences can be drawn from these church songs with regard to women's general participation in sixteenth-century German literature will be considered separately in the Interpretive Essay, below. In remarkable contrast to the first section of this book, each song or group of songs can be introduced by at least some biographical information about the female poet. Astonishingly, no scholars in the fields of theology or musicology, of German literature or Women's Studies have hitherto paid any significant attention to these highly valuable literary documents, and the present translation can only provide first insights into largely unexplored territory. Almost no archival research has been done on any of these female poets; reliable and critical editions of their texts are are yet to be produced. Most of the songs in this book were originally published in a nineteenth-century anthology edited by Philipp Wackernagel, *Das deutsche Kirchenlied* (1864–77).[9]

I. Elisabeth Creutzigerin or Crucigerin

Elisabeth Creutzigerin, née Meseritz, was the first woman in the history of German literature to compose a Protestant church song. She was born around 1500, the daughter of a nobleman in Eastern Pommerania, and joined the Premonstratensian convent at Treptow on the Rega. She learned about Martin Luther's teachings through Johannes Bugenhagen, a fellow Pommeranian who had been school principal in Treptow since 1504 and lecturer in the nearby Premonstratensian monastery Belbuk from 1517 on. In 1521 he began to study in Wittenberg, and soon thereafter he was, upon Luther's strong recommendation, elected minister for the local parish church in that city.[10]

Once Elisabeth had become familiar with Luther's teachings, she quickly desired conversion and escaped her convent in 1522. Bugenhagen welcomed her in his house in Wittenberg, and just two years later, on June 14, 1524, she married Caspar Cruziger the Elder (1504–48).[11] Caspar had been one of Luther's students, was appointed Principal of the St. John's School in Magdeburg in 1525 and Instructor of Theology at the

---

73 (1998): 139–53; Martin H. Jung, " 'Ich habe euch kein Weibergeschwätz geschrieben, sondern das Wort Gottes': Flugschriftenautorinnen der Reformationszeit: Ihr Selbstverständnis im Kontext reformatorischer Theologie," *Luther: Zeitschrift der Luther-Gesellschaft* 69, 1 (1998): 6–18.

9   See above, Introduction, p. 21, n. 56.

10   For an extensive biography, see http://www.bautz.de/bbkl/b/bugenhagen_j.shtml

11   For Elisabeth, see http://www.bautz.de/bbkl/c/cruciger_e.shtml; for Caspar, see http://www.bautz.de/bbkl/c/cruciger_k_d_ae.shtml

University of Wittenberg. He helped Luther in his Bible translations and participated in the famous religious dispute between Luther and Ulrich Zwingli in Marburg in 1529. This dispute led, because the two men could not agree on one essential translation of Christ's words at the Last Supper, to the separation of the Lutheran from the Reformed Church. In 1533 Caspar earned his doctorate in theology and assumed a position at the University of Leipzig where he was especially instrumental in introducing the Protestant Reformation. He edited most of Luther's sermons and collaborated with him in many other areas.

Whereas Caspar worked closely with Luther, his wife Elisabeth was a good friend of Luther's wife, Katharina of Bora, especially as both had formerly been nuns. Luther included Elisabeth's church song 'A Song in Praise of Christ' (*Eyn Lobsanck von Christo*) first in his church songbook *Chorgesangbuch Wittenberg* and his *Erfurter Enchiridion*, both published in 1524, without mentioning her name. Her song met with much approval, as documented in subsequent church songbooks which reprinted her song as well, such as the *Gesangbuch Zwickau* (1525), *Gesangbuch Wittenberg* (1526), and the *Niederdeutsches Gesangbuch* (1526). Beginning with Andreas Rauscher's *Geistliche lieder* (Erfurt 1531), Elisabeth's authorship was no longer suppressed, as documented in Joachim Slüter's *Gesangbuch Rostock* (1531), Hans Walter's *Geystlike leder* (Magdeburg 1534), and Michael Lotther's *Enchiridion Geistliker Leder vnde Psalmen* (Magdeburg 1536). Martin Luther once responded to a theological inquiry by Elisabeth in a letter to her, and he also referred to Elisabeth in some of his *Table Talks*.

On January 19, 1524, a converted Jew, Joachim, sent a reply to Elisabeth from Stettin in which he quoted extensively from her original letter.[12] She had provided him with words of religious encouragement and with the interpretation of some Biblical passages. The Wittenberg student Johann Figulus commented on her wedding to Caspar Crutzinger in a letter dated June 8, 1524, but beyond these witnesses we have no further documents pertaining to this poet. Elisabeth Creutzigerin died in Wittenberg on May 2, 1535.

Elisabeth's hymn, composed probably in 1524, follows,

A Song in Praise of Christ (*Eyn Lobsanck von Christo*)

1. Lord Christ, God's only son
Grew out of the heart
Of his father in eternity,

---

[12]   A copy of the available text can be found in my *'Mein Seel fang an zu singen'*, 265–66.

As it is written [in the New Testament].
He is the Morning Star
Whose brilliant rays extend far
Beyond the other shining stars.

2. He was born for us as a mortal man
At the end of time
To a mother who did not
Lose her virginal chastity.
He lifted the hopelessness of death
He opened Heaven's gates
And returned life to us.

3. Allow us to grow
In Your love and our knowledge of You
So that we continue to stay in our belief
And provide You such spiritual service
So that we can taste here on Earth
Your sweetness in the heart
And feel thirsty after You all the time.

4. You creator of all things
You fatherly power,
You rule from the beginning to the end [of time][13]
Drawing strength from Your own might.
Make our heart turn toward You
And blind our physical senses[14]
So that they do not go astray from You.

5. Give us death through Your goodness!
Awaken us through Your grace!
Subdue the old creature in us,[15]
So as to give life to the new one!
May this happen, while we still live,
To our senses and all our [physical] desires
So that we have cause to give You our thanks.

II. Mary Queen of Hungary

Mary, later Queen of Hungary, was born in Brussels on September 17, 1505, the daughter of Philip of Burgundy and his wife Joanna. She was

---

[13] Literally: 'from end to end.'
[14] Literally: 'and turn away our senses.'
[15] The poet says only: 'make the old creature sick,' but we can safely assume that the mystical message implies the metaphysical death of the old human body.

the sister of Emperor Charles V (1500–58) under whose rule the Hapsburg empire saw its widest extension ever. On January 13, 1522, Mary married the very young King Louis II (Lajos) of Hungary, who was just sixteen years old. Although the parents had arranged this marriage, Mary and Louis seem to have enjoyed a passionate love relationship. Tragically, when Louis died in the devastating battle against the victorious Turks at Mohács on August 29, 1526, his young widow had to flee from Budapest and fell into deep depression, deciding never to marry again.

Mary enjoyed many indirect contacts with Martin Luther, who dedicated some of his exegetical writings to her and exchanged with her a number of letters. Similarly, the famous humanist Erasmus of Rotterdam dedicated his *Vidua christiana* (1529) to her.[16] Although Mary remained a steadfast Catholic throughout her life, she obviously felt greatly attracted to the Protestant Reformation and made many efforts to negotiate between both Churches. On July 5, 1531, she assumed, on behalf of her brother Emperor Charles V, the government of the Netherlands and ruled this Hapsburgian province successfully until 1555, protecting it from the French kings (House of Valois), who eagerly tried to acquire this Northern territory. On the one hand Mary often consulted with many Dutch (Protestant) councillors, permitting them to gain considerable political influence; on the other she enacted all those imperial edicts coming from her brother Charles which were aimed at fending off the Protestant cause. On October 25, 1555, Mary resigned from her post and retired to Spain, where she died on October 18, 1558, in Cigales near Valladolid.[17]

Mary's song "MAg ich Unglück nicht widerstan" was often included in Protestant church songbooks, although she herself never converted to Protestantism. And many times over the centuries editors clearly identified her as the poet of this song, from as early as in the *Magdeburger niederdeutsches Gesangbuch* of 1534 to as late as in Eybe Johann of Spreckesen's *Zwey-Stimmiges Vollständiges Evangelisches Lutherisches Chorahl-Buch nach dem Neuen Stader-Gesang-Buch* of 1752. Modern scholarship, however, has repeatedly voiced some doubts about her

---

[16]   Albrecht Classen and Tanya Amber Settle, "Women in Martin Luther's Life and Theology," *German Studies Review* XIV, 2 (1991): 231–60, here 253–54.

[17]   Albert F[riedrich] W[ilhelm] Fischer, *Kirchenlieder-Lexikon. Hymnologisch-literarische Nachweisungen über ca. 450 der wichtigsten und verbreitetsten Kirchenlieder aller Zeiten in alphabetischer Folge nebst einer Übersicht der Liederdichter*, 2 vols. (Gotha: Friedrich Andreas Pertes, 1879; rpt. Hildesheim: Georg Olms, 1967), here vol. 1, 455; for a recent biography, see Ursula Tamussino, *Maria von Ungarn. Ein Lebensbild im Dienst der Casa de Austria* (Graz, Vienna, and Cologne: Verlag Styria, 1998).

authorship, with reference to her social rank and the Protestant orientation of her song. But a close reading of the text reveals that her name has been woven into the first lines of each stanza: MARIA. All attempts to identify Martin Luther, or any other male poet, as the possible composer have utterly failed, especially as any one of them would probably have signed the song by name.

Mary's hymn, composed probably in 1526, follows.

Mag ich Unglück nicht widerstan

1. I cannot fight against misfortune.
I must suffer from disgrace
Coming from the world because of my true belief.
But I know, it is my art,
God's grace and mercy
Which people must acknowledge.
God is not far away,
He is just hiding
For a short time
Until He strangles those
Who deprive me of His words.

2. Now I must arrange my affairs
Because I am weak
And God allows me to experience fear.
Nevertheless, I know that no power is permanent;
The best would be
If everything temporal would disappear.
The eternal values
Provide the right attitude.
I'll stick to this,
And risk my body and goods,
May God help me to overcome the enemies.

3. As the proverb says: everything requires its own time for maturation.
Lord Jesus Christ
You will [I trust] stand at my side
And consider my misfortune
As if it were Your own
When I am under assault
Once I'll have to take my own path,
Oh world, do as it pleases you,
God will be my shield;
He will certainly accompany me. Amen.

III. Agnes, Duchess of Saxony

Agnes (1527–55) was the daughter of the Hessian Landgrave Philipp the Magnanimous (der Großmütige) (1504–65). In 1541 she married Moritz, Elector of Saxony, with whom she lived for twelve years, until he died in 1553. In that year Agnes composed an important poem of mourning and political reflection, "ACh Gott, an einem morgen,"[18] in which she identifies herself through an acrostic: *AGNes HerrZogIn Zu SAchSen ChurFurStin* ('Agnes, Duchess and Elector of Saxony'). Her poem is a moving expression of her personal grief and also a remarkable poetic creation in literary terms. Agnes's first husband was a strong defender of the Protestant Church, as was she.

Two years later she married Johann Friedrich II, Duke of Saxony-Gotha (May 26, 1555), but she died in the same year, on November 4.

1. Oh God, one day in the morning
I saw a bier in my dream:
I was afraid of great sorrow
Which later afflicted me indeed.
  Now here they bring my dead husband
[Who died] in the best time of our life,[19]
This brings mighty lamentation and sorrow.

2. My God, he had often
Been burdened with great labor and danger,
In his young days
He often pursued the enemy.
  He attacked them very forcefully
To bring peace for Germany,
All of them were afraid of him.[20]

3. Finally, the Margrave
Caused great misery in Germany
With killing and burning.[21]
My husband fought against him.

---

[18]   Quoted from Philipp Wackernagel, ed., *Das deutsche Kirchenlied von der ältesten Zeit bis zu Anfang des XVII. Jahrhunderts*, vol. 4, p. 1102, no. 1573.

[19]   Verbatim: 'in our best years.'

[20]   Literally: 'everybody was afraid of him.'

[21]   Agnes refers to the military events in the Schmalkaldic War, 1547–1548, in which the Protestant League fought against the Catholic Emperor Charles V. The reference to the Margrave is probably to Elector Johann Friedrich of Saxony, who was captured and defeated on April 24, 1547. For extensive genealogical information about the Elector and his family, see http://genealogy.euweb.cz/wettin/wettin11.html; Bodo Nischan, "Germany after 1550," *The Reformation World*, ed. Andrew Pettegree (London and New York: Routledge, 2000), 387–409.

He went to battle, accompanied by the men of his country,
And devoutly defeated the enemy:
Oh Lord, that cost him his life's blood!

4. The victory is accompanied by heavy sorrow
For me and my dear child!
Oh, what use are big walls
When we are made orphans [and widows]![22]
    As I consider his life and death
While I yet live
I must lament about it to God!

5. My own life and the Electorship
And all the land
I would have given up for him!
Alas, wishing does not help:
    Now God must be my guardian,
I commend myself to him entirely
In God alone I trust.

IV. Annelein of Freiburg

In 1583 a church songbook appeared in print with the title *Außbund* ('Bundle of Songs') which also contained a poem by the hitherto unknown Annelein of Freiburg. The anonymous editor introduces her song stating: "Another song by Annelein of Freiburg; she was drowned in 1529 and then her body was burned." Was she accused of witchcraft, or was she a martyr for the Protestant cause? At this point nothing is known about her, but we can be certain that she was a deeply religious person and composed at least more than a single church song. Her execution in 1529 by drowning indicates that she had to undergo an ordeal designed to find out whether she was a witch. Obviously she failed the test, perhaps because her body kept floating after she had drowned, and subsequently her corpse was burned. But the song implies that she died for her belief.

Oh God, protect my heart and mouth (*O Gott, bewar mein hertz vnd mund*), after the melody of *In dich hab ich gehoffet, Herr* (My trust I have placed in you, oh Lord)

1. Eternal Father in Heaven
I call upon You passionately

---

[22] Literally she uses the specific term for 'orphaned,' but since she refers to herself as well, we need to add the expression 'and widows.'

Do not allow me to turn away from you.
Keep me in Your truth
Until the end of my life!

2. Oh God, protect my heart and mouth!
Lord, guard me continually,
Let me not depart from you,
Whether it be in sorrow, fear, or misery,
Protect me pure in [my] joy!

3. My eternal Lord, You my Father,
I am a poor and unworthy child,
Give me direction and teaching
That I may know Your paths and ways:
That is what I am longing for.

4. To walk through death with the help of Your strength,
Through sorrow, torture, fear, and misery:
I beg you to protect me in all these [dangers]
So that I will never be separated
Oh Lord, from Your love.

5. Many take this path
Where there is the cup of suffering,
And also [the cup] of many false teachings
Which seek to make us turn away
From Christ, our Lord.

6. To You, oh Lord, I lift my soul,
I place all my hope in You in case of danger
Protect me from being dishonored,
That my enemies here on Earth
May not triumph over me.

7. They keep me as a prisoner:
Oh God, with all my heart I am waiting for You
With burning desire,
For the day when You will wake up
And free Your [children] who are in prison.[23]

8. Oh God Father, in Your kingdom
Make us like the five virgins

---

[23]   This line requires conjecture, as it says verbatim: 'and free Your prisoners,' although the
first line of this stanza (seven) indicates that the narrative voice means that she is impris-
oned by earthly enemies.

Who were very prudent,
Patiently waiting for the groom
And his selected host.

9. Eternal King of the Heavenly Kingdom,
Give us food and drink forever
In the form of truthful nourishment
Which will never be spoiled
In the way of all spiritual matter.

10. If You withdraw Your nourishment from us
Then everything will be lost and [all effort] will have been in vain,
Without You we can achieve nought:
Because of Your grace we place our hope in You,
We will not fail in this.

11. I have no doubt of God's power
His judgments are truthful,
He will not abandon anyone
Who is strong and steady in her belief
And stays on the right path.[24]

12. Be confident, you Christians, and cheerful
Through Jesus Christ in eternity,
He gives us love and belief,
God gives us consolation through His holy words
In which we should have trust.

13. I commend myself to God and his host,
Today He will be my leader
Because of His name:
This You will do, my Father,
On behalf of Jesus Christ, Amen.

V. Elisabeth, Duchess of Brunswick-Calenberg

Duchess Elisabeth of Brunswick-Calenberg (1510–58), the daughter of
the Duke Elector Joachim I of Brandenburg (1484–1535) and his wife
Elisabeth (1485–1555), composed fifteen songs between the years 1553
and 1555. In 1525, when she was only fourteen years old, she married
Eric I of Brunswick-Calenberg (1470–1540), who was forty years

---

[24] Annelein explicitly utilizes the feminine singular for the genitive singular pronoun "der,"
but then switches, in the following line, to the gender-neutral "das."

older than herself and cared little about his family and his country. When he died in 1540, Elisabeth was suddenly confronted with huge state debts and had to run the country on behalf of her under-age son Eric II (1528–84). Influenced by Antonius Corvinus,[25] Elisabeth, who had converted in 1538, introduced Protestantism in her territory between 1542 and 1543. To strengthen the new Church, she drafted a policy, *Christliche Kirchen Ordnung*, which was printed in Erfurt in 1542, and reprinted in the Low German dialect in Hanover in 1544. In 1546 Elisabeth handed over the government to her son and married Poppo XVIII, Count of Henneberg (1513–74), on May 30, 1546. To her chagrin, her son reverted to Catholicism and experienced serious political and religious conflicts with the neighboring territories where Protestantism reigned supreme. Most problematic proved to be a guarantee that Elisabeth had given for a major loan to the city of Hanover which, however, could not repay the money. Consequently Elisabeth was thrown into prison until her son-in-law, Duke Albrecht of Prussia (1490–1568), who had married her second daughter Anna Maria (1532–68), came to her rescue and secured the necessary funds.

Most of Elisabeth's songs date from this difficult time. She mostly relied on older songs and contrafacted them, that is, she composed new texts to well-known melodies. In 1555 Elisabeth also wrote a widow's guidebook, *Widwen Handbuechlein Durch eine Hocherleucht Fuerstliche Widwe*, which was printed in 1556 and reprinted five more times up to 1609.[26] Here three songs will serve to represent Elisabeth's poetic oeuvre.

No. 2: A Prayer for Help (*Ein Gebet um Hilfe*), composed on Friday after Michaelmas, 1554

1. Oh God my Lord, consider this
And have mercy on me.
How few are they who believe in You.
Poor me, I am forlorn.
They do not pay attention to Your words.
Among these god-forsaken folks
There is no more belief to be found.

---

[25] For a biography of Corvinus, see http://www.bautz.de/bbkl/c/corvinus_a.shtml
[26] Texts quoted from Goltz, Freiherr von der Goltz-Greifswald, "Lieder der Herzogin Elisabeth von Braunschweig-Lüneburg, Gräfin von Henneberg zu Hannover von 1553 bis 1555 gedichtet," *Zeitschrift der Gesellschaft für niedersächsische Kirchengeschichte* 19 (1914): 147–208; see also Konrad Ameln, "Ein Lied der Herzogin Elisabeth von Calenberg-Göttingen im Tod 'Innsbruck, ich muß dich lassen'," *Jahrbuch der Gesellschaft für niedersächsische Kirchengeschichte* 90 (1992): 267–71.

2. Oh God my Lord, they have no intention
Of promoting Your honor and Your words,
They only pretend to be God-fearing.
They think they can destroy Your words.
Therefore, please, eliminate them all
So that Your honor and words remain true,
And this is what they truly hate the most.

3. Oh God my Lord, how has all obedience
Here on Earth been abandoned!
Loyalty, love, and truth do no longer count
Here on Earth.
Those who do not believe in God are in the majority,
Which so many a pious person laments
But against which one cannot fight.

4. Oh God my Lord, it is true what they say:
Who would dare to oppose us.
We are now powerful and control the laws.
Nobody can defy us.
Whatever we do represents the common norm
Inasmuch as the Antichrist stands by us
And helps us with money to stay in power.

5. Oh God my Lord, they are truly convinced
That they control all power here on Earth,
Whatever they say constitutes the general law.
You should stand up against them
And destroy their great superciliousness.
They will not be able to fight against You,
You will always be God here on Earth.

6. Oh God my Lord, please be prepared
To rescue me and Your other subjects.
May my lament reach Your ear!
May You hear my prayer!
Let actions follow in response to our belief
And attack them violently
To increase Your praise and honor.

7. Oh God my Lord, You have verily tested me [and found in me a true believer][27]

---

[27] This extra half line is probably the combination of verb and predicate adverb ("prüuest mich woll"), directly leading to the second verse. One must assume an omission of some sort in the transmission.

By continuing to grant me Your grace.
You have found me completely sincere in my belief.
I will not give up my hope in Your words.[28]
I love them and enjoy listening to them,
For that reason I endure the enmity of those who do not believe in God,
Though [the words] shine in this country.

8. Oh God my Lord, keep me pure,
And do not make me accept the advice of the non-believers
Who admonish me to destroy Your true teaching.
Do not grant them this triumph.
Raise, oh Lord, Your resistance
And let me be commended to You
Together with all other believers.

9. Oh God my Lord, the fools actually say
That there is no God on Earth.
Might conquers right
Which I constantly lament.
Your words, loyalty, and truth do not count,
Instead everything that the godless think has priority,
I hope, oh God, You will oppose them.

10. Oh God my Lord, what shall I further lament?
Your words have become a matter
Of foolishness and great contempt for them
Which will prove to be their loss, as they will find out.
Your servants do not count anything among them.
They treat God the Lord
As they treat, oh God, the slaves.[29]

11. Oh God my Lord, the time for prayer has come,
For the devil is full of hatred and envy,
He would like to hurl me into misery.
But I think that God sees everything,
Therefore I always watch out for the devil
Not to allow him to take possession of anything of mine
Because You have [already] overcome him.

12. Oh God my Lord I am waiting for You,
I am confident and do not despair,
Whatever You say, it will come true;
I will never doubt this.

---

[28] Elisabeth refers to God's words in the singular.
[29] Literally: 'farmhands.'

When I shout [for help] You rescue me,
Your merciful ears hear me,
This I want to believe without any shred of doubt.

13. Oh God my Lord, I trust in You,
My belief will not deceive me,
Though there are still great dangers
Which You cannot yet prevent for me,
Since there is no defense against the army of devils.[30]
Once this time and several more years will have passed,
The new [promised] time will soon arrive.

14. Oh God my Lord, open their eyes
And show them their sinfulness.
Make them recognize their great folly
In their persecuting me.
Then people will freely talk about it
That God gives illumination without hurting us.
Praised be those who trust in Him.

15. Oh God my Lord, I further request from You,
—You can surely grant me this—
That I will be able to love my enemies from the bottom of my heart
And forgive them completely.
God, forgive them also in this instant.
But if You do not, then wreak Your revenge
To which only You are entitled.

16. Oh God my Lord, when I am failing
And do not have guidance,
Then my eyes turn to You,
You will certainly find the solution.
Do not reject me in my old age,
Do not leave me alone when my hair turns grey,
While I sing the praise of Your grace.

17. Oh God my Lord, help me in my endeavor,
May my hope not be deceived,
To announce Your might in public
To the children of children and their descendants
So that they learn to fear You,
That they do not disregard Your command.
Grant them Your grace to realize this.

---

[30] Lines 4 and 5 are not fully understandable and defy a simple translation.

18. Oh God my Lord, herewith I come to an end,
Please include me in Your grace,
Spare me from Your grim punishment.
Let the poor innocent people here on Earth
Be entrusted to Your grace,
And likewise all those who love and honor You
And do not be loath to grant them Your love, Amen.

    All honor to God alone, Amen.

No. 8: A Greeting on New Year's Eve (*Ein Neujahrsgruß*),
First Advent of 1554

1. God alone in the highest be given honor,
And thanks for His grace.
He has given me the little sweet girl Catharina
Mercifully as my daughter.
Her life is completely guided by respect for Him,[31]
She is truly decorated with her love for God,
For the praise and honor of the Lord.

2. I thank God for this in all eternity
And praise His grace
From which I have received a great gift.
Infinite praise be to Him.
His grace helps me carry the heavy cross[32]
And does not allow the world to abandon me[33]—
For which the Lord is willing to give her a reward.

3. Oh Jesus Christ, the only son
Of Your heavenly father,
Have mercy on the abandoned orphan
For the sake of her obedience.
Give a pious marriage partner to her who fears You,
Bless her with a long life
As You are God and Father of the orphans.

4. Oh Holy Spirit, You good consoler,
You most healing consoler,
Give her strength henceforth through the fear of God,

---

[31]   The original has 'she lives in fear of Him.'

[32]   The poet refers to His grace in the third person singular feminine: 'She helps me carry the heavy cross.'

[33]   This line requires conjecture since it reads literally: 'It does not allow the world to turn away.'

To stay piously with Christ.
She does not love anybody more here on Earth
But You and me, my Lord and God,
This she will not repent.

5. I praise, honor, and worship You.[34]
She is growing up in the love of God;
She despises arrogance and luxury;
She strives to fulfill my and Your will,
Therefore, my God and Lord, give her Your blessing,
And be her Lord and Father at all times,
Here and for ever, Amen.

Dear child, follow the orders
Of your mother, I advise you,
Do not submit to the temptations of the world;
Love me and honor God the Lord;
Let this become true in you;
This I wish you for the New Year.

No. 12: A Marriage Song (*Ein Hochzeitslied*) (Monday after Estomihi[35] 1555)

1. Take note, pious Christianity
As you are standing in the words of God,
The person who keeps the word in His heart and learns it
Will gain great honor here on Earth and in the afterlife.

2. See, there comes the noble lord and duke
Who always thirsts for God's teachings,
He brings an honest and fine young lady,
The Lord's blessing will be with her.

3. Good friend, this will be to your profit
That you have married this young lady,
She shines with honorable virtues,
God will certainly bless you spiritually.

4. Stay in His belief and live in harmony,
Then God will give fertility,[36]

---

[34] Elisabeth here differentiates between the Godhead and her own daughter through the personal pronoun.

[35] 'Esto mihi in deum protectorem'(Be for me as a protector god, Ps. 71,3). This refers to the specific reading during mass on the seventh sunday before Easter.

[36] Literally, 'fruit of your body.'

Children will surround you
As olive trees, healthy and fresh.

5. Praise and honor be given to the Lord
Who keeps us safely in His kingdom.
Praise him for his munificence
Sing in His honor and use this melody.

6. May God give, through the Lord Jesus Christ,
A good life to bride and bridegroom,
May you live in respect and honor,
Fully in fear of God.[37] Amen.

The poet concludes her song with a statement in prose: "Whoever wins a wife receives a good thing and will create something good and be loved by the Lord."

VI. Magdalena Bekin

Frequently church songbooks contain songs by women whose biography remains entirely unknown to us. Around 1560, for instance, the highly regarded Nuremberg printer Hans Koler published Magdalena Bekin's song *Mag es dann je nit anders gsein* in his anthology *Vierzehen schoene Geystliche Lieder* ('Fourteen Beautiful Spiritual Songs').[38] In 1569 he also copied this song in his *Hundert christenlichen Hausgesengen* ('Hundred Christian Songs for the Home Service'). Other collectors of church songs too included Bekin's composition; one such was Nicolaus Selnecker, who published his church hymn book *Christliche Psalmen, Lieder, vnd Kirchengesenge* ('Christian Psalms, Songs, and Churchsongs') in Leipzig in 1587. Magdalena's song obviously enjoyed considerable popularity and was widely reprinted at least up to 1648, but we do not know anything about her life in any specific terms.[39] Her name is documented through an acrostic: MAgDaLeNA BekIn.

---

[37]   Literally: 'entirely surrendered into God's power.'

[38]   The suffix 'in' means that she was married to a man called 'Becke' or 'Beke,' which probably indicates that he was a baker. Some modern translators drop the suffix to adjust the name to modern usage and to be politically correct, but this contradicts late-medieval and early-modern usage; see also note 42 below.

[39]   Philipp Wackernagel, *Das deutsche Kirchenlied*, vol. 4, no. 719, p. 527; see also Julius Mützell, ed., *Geistliche Lieder der Evangelischen Kirche aus dem sechszehnten* (sic) *Jahrhundert, nach den ältesten Drucken*, 3 vols. (Berlin: Th. Chr. Fr. Enslin, 1855), vol. 2, 611.

Can there never be any alternative? (*Mag es dann je nicht anders gsein?*)

1. Can there never be any alternative?
Oh God, have mercy on me!
Am I the only one who experiences misfortune today?
Lord, take me into Your protection
And turn away from me
Through Your divine grace
The cross that I have to bear.
Lord, You know well what it takes.

2. After all, Lord, whomever You attack
And whomever You deny Your help,
Would not be able to resist You.
I beg You, do not forsake me.
How often have I heard,
Through Your divine word,
That You will never abandon the person
Who trusts in You.

3. Calm Your wrath and strengthen in me
The belief, Lord, this is my desire.
I beg you by Your divine grace
To forgive me my sins
Which I have so often
Committed in so many an action[40]
Against You:
oh Lord, be merciful to me.

4. Moreover, Lord, I am ready to carry the cross,
If You do not want to spare me from it.
All I request from You is that You stand by me
That I may accept it with patience.
High-born Lord,
Let go Your wrath,
Grant me patience,
Truly, I admit, my sins are the cause of Your wrath.[41]

5. All my hope rests in You, my God,
I will be deeply in sin until my death,
Which causes me great suffering, fear, and misery,
Against which You provide good help and advice.

---

[40] Literally: 'on many extensive journeys.'
[41] Literally: 'Truly, it is the fault of my sins.'

Therefore I lament to You,
I beg You not to hold back
Your help,
Otherwise I would have to be sad forever.

6. If I confess my sins to You
And repent them deep in my heart,
Then it will be as You have promised,
Forgotten and forgiven.
Your words are true,
Pure, honest, and clear
As sunshine for the person
Who trusts in them with the full heart.

7. In God I place my joy,
Which is the result of His divine word alone.
Lord, determine everything according to Your will.
You alone can give me patience.
You are my consolation
As You have redeemed me
Through Your blood.
That is the [true] joy of a Christian.

In Nicolaus Selnecker's songbook of 1587 Magdalena's song continues with two additional stanzas, although we do not know whether they come from the poet herself or were composed by someone else. But there is no apparent reason to assume that these two stanzas were not Magdalena's own creation:

8. I entrust myself to Your hands;
Lord Jesus, I will die and live for You.
With all my heart I long for You, oh God,
Stand by me when death approaches.
Good-bye, good-bye,
I am going into Heaven
By agency of Christ's blood,
Now I have won eternity.

9. No shame, dishonor, sword, or death will stop me;
Christ is the only hero in this life.
Temporal life falls away from me,
Christ offers me eternal life.
What else might I want?
Death, now come,
I am willing
In this way I go on living.

VII. Magdalena Heymairin

The case of Magdalena Heymairin might be the most unusual in the history of late-medieval and early-modern German women's literature, as she was a schoolteacher and composed many of her texts with pedagogical purposes in mind.[42] In the prologue to her 'Sunday Epistles' (*Sontegliche Epistel*, 1561) she reports that she taught Katharina of Degenwart's two daughters in Straubing, located on the Danube southeast of Regensburg. She herself hailed from Regensburg and married the schoolteacher Heymair who worked in Cham (northeastern Bavaria). In 1564 a conflict erupted in Cham which had been inherited by Prince Elector Frederick III of the Palatinate in 1559. Frederick adhered to Calvinism and wanted to introduce his religion in Cham. For this purpose he gave a school charter to a Calvinist teacher, Veit Wurzer, although Magdalena and her husband protested against this professional competition. Cham was too small a city to support two schools, as Magdalena pointed out in a letter to the School District Supervisor Nikolaus Gallus in Regensburg dated February 16, 1570. But all their efforts were for naught, and around 1571 the couple were forced to leave Cham and settle in Regensburg. Possibly, Magdalena's husband died soon thereafter as we hear only from her after that date. In 1585 she was living in Grafenwerth in Austria, and was appointed Court Steward in the household of the widow Judith Reuber, née Fridensheim, in Kaschau. Nothing else is presently known about Magdalena's life and work.

She published the following major works: *Die Sontegliche Epistel* ('Sunday Epistles', 1561), *Die Apostel Geschichte* ('The Apostolic Account', 1573); *Das Buechlein Jesu Syrachs* ('The Book of Jesus Syrach', 1578), *Das geistliche A.B.C.* ('The Spiritual ABC', no year); and *Das Buoch Tobiae* ('The Book of Tobias', 1586).[43]

---

[42] Again, the suffix 'in' implies that she is the wife of Heymair; it was standard practice in the late Middle Ages to identify married women in this way, for example, Ottilia Fenchlerin, Clara Hätzlerin, Maria Beckin. See also note 37 above. It was not quite unusual to find women as teachers, particularly in women convents and beguine courts: see Walter Simons, *Cities of Ladies. Beguine Communities in the Medieval Low Countries, 1200–1565*, The Middle Ages Series (Philadelphia: University of Pennsylvania Press, 2001), 80–85. But we do not yet know much about secular women teachers such as Heymairin. Maya Bijvoet Williamson, *The Memoirs of Helene Kottanner (1439–1440)*, trans. from the German with Introduction, Interpretive Essay and Notes, Library of Medieval Women (Cambridge: D. S. Brewer, 1998), consistently drops the 'in' suffix, whereas the German keeps it as a natural part of the proper name.

[43] Cornelia Niekus Moore, "Biblische Weisheiten für die Jugend. Die Schulmeisterin Magdalena Heymair," *Deutsche Literatur von Frauen*, Vol. 1: *Vom Mittelalter bis zum Ende des 18. Jahrhunderts*, ed. Gisela Brinker-Gabler (Munich: Beck, 1988), 172–84;

I have selected as a representative piece Magdalena's 'The Spiritual ABC', although it is impossible to imitate the alphabetic arrangement in the English translation. In the original, each stanza is introduced with a word that provides the respective letter in the alphabet. The original first word in each stanza for the alphabetical sequence is reproduced here in bold face.

1. [**AN**] person here on Earth
Should live without fear of God:
If you want to acquire reason,
Turn your heart to the Lord.
He gives you good advice,
He teaches you in all things,
So that you will succeed in everything
And will not experience any suffering.

2. [**BItt**] Request from God without any horror[44]
That He may help you in time of need,
Give Him your full confidence,
Since He is your beloved God
Who can quickly come to your assistance.
Otherwise you will perish here on Earth
And suffer death in eternity
Because of your sin.

3. [**CReützig**] Submit your body to God in his praise,
Be obedient and quiet,
Live in the way of the Holy Spirit,
Do not do what your flesh desires,
Rather live according to the model of the Spirit
And resist [the temptation] of your flesh,
So you can live forever
In praise and honor of God.

4. [**DEmuetigkeit**] Practice humility
Which pleases God very much.
Love everything that is just
So you will enjoy honor.
Be merciful,
So that Christ can say,

Cornelia Niekus Moore, *The Maiden's Mirror. Reading Material for German Girls in the Sixteenth and Seventeenth Centuries*, Wolfenbütteler Forschungen, 36 (Wiesbaden: Harrassowitz, 1987).

44   Magdalena indeed uses the word "grawen" ('horror') instead of "forcht" ('fear'), as in the first line of the first stanza.

To the dismay of your enemies,
'Come to me, my beloved creatures.'

5. [**EHr**] Give honor to God and serve him with your full heart,
Follow His teachings,
He does not tolerate any folly.
He likes nothing more than
That which His beloved Son
Has given us as His law:
Let all the evil people rage as they wish,
God is still sitting on the highest throne.

6. [**FÖrcht**] Fear God above all things
As He can lead body and soul
To condemnation
And into the torture of Hell.
No person here on Earth can accomplish this.
Oh man, you better strive
To love God above everything else
Since He is worthy of this honor.

7. [**GAr**] Pay very close attention
That you do not bear your cross here on Earth
Without being selected for it.
You want to be worthy for the Lord
And stay with Him forever.
To do so you have to suffer with Him,
Avoid the joys of this world
In accordance with His words.

8. [**HAlt**] Keep peace with everyone
And love your neighbor.
If your love is to please Him
Then it has to come out of your heart.
Christ will let know those [whom He identifies thus:],
'Even if you do not name yourself,
You will be recognized as those
Who are my disciples.'

9. [**IN**] When you experience fear and great suffering
Rely on God
Then you will continue to experience joy.
Do not pay attention to the mockery of the world
Think of the state of blessedness.
Disgrace [suffering] here in this life

Is not worth any consideration, think only
Of the joys of the future.

10. **[KEhr]** Turn all your heart, mind, and senses
To your God alone,
Then you will realize,
And believe in this (I am not joking)
That God your Father
On His high throne
And with His Holy Spirit and Son
Will always stand by you.

11. **[LEhrn]** From Christ learn this teaching,
He is truth Himself.
Give Him all the honor due to Him,
Do not apply the tricks of those who deceive.
Trust His words alone
Since from the Father's lap
Comes forward Christ's teaching—
As all of God's servants say.

12. **[MIt]** Together with all pious Christians
Have joy in God alone.
Reject the false philosophers here on Earth.
Don't join their community.
The person who has to suffer now
Sadness here in this life,
You should not leave alone.
Instead help him to bear his suffering.

13. **[NIcht]** Do not allow wrath and great envy
To gain control of you.
Be peaceful, as a solution will be found,
Heed Christ's example:
When they vituperated him,
He did not defend himself,
But he contradicted them
And insisted on his own teaching.

14. **[OPffer]** Sacrifice yourself for God
Who has created you.
Do not keep hidden his words,
Instead strive by day and night
That you fully live according to them
Without deception and shame,
Even if the world were making you
To suffer a hard bitter death.

15. [**PAulus**] St. Paul says, hand yourself over
To divine council,
Like the fellow sufferers of Christ
Who suffer here, but in His grace.
God's pure children
Who want to avoid all sins
Must accept much suffering.
To this you must resign yourself.

16. [**QVaelle(n)**] God will painfully torture the hearts
Of all those
Who will not live with all their heart
According to Christ's teaching.
Protect yourself from the advice
Given by those people
Who hang their coat as the wind blows[45]
As you can see it by day and night.

17. [**RIcht**] Give fair judgment and say: 'it is up to God to decide'
Then you will earn honor.
Whether you are young or old,
Always follow His model.
Do not issue false judgment
About your neighbor
And his Christian lifestyle.
Instead, closely watch your tongue.

18. [**SElig**] Blessed may you be in the Lord
When the evil world
Hurts you and your honor
And thinks the worst of you.
Keep in mind what Christ says,
That you are separated from the world
And that it cannot hurt you.
Follow this advice.[46]

19. [**THuo**] Do good in the community,
Do not let any burden frighten you,
Do not abandon any friend
Who has done good to you.
Also love your enemies
Who craftily scheme
How they might bring you down
And cause you fear and pain.

---

[45] In modern terms: 'those who are opportunists.'
[46] Literally: 'judgment.'

20. **[VNglauben]** Stay away from disbelief[47]
As it encompasses all sins.
Believe in Christ and be filled with joy,
A joy that characterizes God's children.
Stay away from such advice
As is given by those who mock the Lord
And fail to believe in the Commandments
That he had issued.

21. **[WAch]** Wake up and do not sleep
Prepare yourself with all your might.
Death pursues its own plans.
Request from God that He will
Help you in haste
So that you can, according to His will,
Be prepared for him steadfastly
Until your last hour arrives.

22. **[XEll]** Do not associate with those people
Who are hypocrites in the face of God
Who continually
Cause distress for the pious believers.
May you not be misled by them
As they can easily flatter you
And deceive foe and friend.
God will punish these beasts.

23. **[YSt]** When Christ is in your heart
When you know His words
Do not attempt to deceive Him
Instead thank Him for this promise.[48]
The treasure and the grace
Are not given to everyone.
Be humble in your life,
Give help and advice to your neighbor.

24. **[ZV]** We all will have to face
Christ's Day of Judgment.
When you then will be able
To recite this ABC correctly
And without any lamentation
And if you will have lived according to its teachings

---

[47] Alternatively: 'lack of belief.'
[48] Literally: 'pawn.'

You will enjoy the fruits of it.
The enemy will be furious
When you will enter God's realm.

VIII. Margaretha, Duchess of Anhalt

Margaretha (1473–1530) was the daughter of the Duke of Münsterberg and was married to Duke Ernst of Anhalt, whom she had married in 1494. Her husband died in 1516, but she lived for a further fourteen years. Margaretha was active as a poet, but her extensive rhymed 'History of the Suffering, Dying, Resurrection, and Ascension of Christ' appeared in print as late as twenty-three years posthumously in 1553, published by the printer Wolff Günter in Leipzig.

After Duke Ernst's death, Margaretha took on the responsibilities of government on behalf of her under-age children. In this role she rigorously fought against the Protestant Reformation from 1520 on and polemicized against it in her poems and other texts, although she had previously had some contacts with Martin Luther (1483–1546)[49] himself and the humanist, teacher, court preacher, and reformer Georg Spalatin (1484–1545).[50] Her change of heart was due to the influence of the court preacher, the Dominican monk Johannes Mensing. Margaretha even went so far as to support important representatives of the Catholic Church who bitterly fought against the Reformation, Hieronymus Emser (1478–1527)[51] and Johannes Cochläus (1479–1552).[52] Her *Historia*, a version in rhymed verse of the Sermon of the Mount, also reflects her religious struggles, along with some prayers, and some other religious poems. Margaretha's son, Duke Georg (1507–1553), had his mother's *Historia* printed in honor of her memory, though, in an epilogue, he criticized some of the infelicities in the rhyme structure.[53] Here I translate only the first section concerning Vespers.[54]

---

[49] http://www.bautz.de/bbkl/l/luther_m.shtml
[50] http://www.bautz.de/bbkl/s/spalatin_g.shtml
[51] http://www.bautz.de/bbkl/e/emser_h.shtml
[52] http://www.bautz.de/bbkl/c/cocchlaeus_j.shtml
[53] Quoted from Philipp Wackernagel, ed., *Das deutsche Kirchenlied*, vol. 4, no. 1551, 1072–83.
[54] Vespers is the sixth of the Canonical Hours of the Breviary, i.e., the evening hour, either 5 o'clock or 6 o'clock, see http://www.newadvent.org/cathen/15381a.htm; the best source for medieval and early-modern measurement of time still is Otto Grotefend, *Taschenbuch der Zeitrechnung des deutschen Mittelalters und der Neuzeit*, 11th, improved, ed. by Th. Ulrich (Hanover: Hahn, 1971), 23; an updated and expanded version is available online at http://www.manuscripta-mediaevalia.de/gaeste/grotefend/grotefend.htm

Historia vom Leiden, Sterben, Auferstehung und Himelfart Christi

1. Lord God, think of helping me, let me see a sign of Your help,
So that I may be able to see the suffering of Your son
The suffering he had to accept at the Hour of Vespers
Through which he freed us from our sins.

2. Jesus Christ's suffering began
When he went from Bethany to Jerusalem
And sat at the table with His twelve Apostles
And wanted to eat with them the Easter lamb.

3. He said: "I have long desired to eat this little lamb
Together with you, my dear disciples, as a symbol of my suffering.
But one of you will be my traitor
And will hand me over to my enemies."

4. The disciples were very frightened, and each said to the Lord:
"Is it me, Lord, who will be responsible for doing it?"
"Master, is it me?," asked Judas, "this I ask."
Jesus said: "You are saying it yourself."

5. Among the disciples fighting broke out about who would be the greatest.
The Lord got up from the table and undressed.
Then he poured water into a basin
And washed their feet and afterwards wiped them clean.

6. He said: "You call me Master, and that's what I am, Your Lord,
I have washed your feet and am kneeling in front of you on the floor.
With this I have given you an example
For you to live in humility and love."

7. As soon as the Lord sat down again at the table,
He took the bread in His hand and blessed it:
"Take and eat, this is my body, think of Him
Who will be turned over to death for you."

8. He took the cup filled with wine in His hand,
He blessed it, thanking God His Father:
"Take the cup and drink [the wine] as my blood,
Which will be spilled for the many sinners."

9. With His mind deeply grieved, He said to them: "I tell you verily,
One among you twelve disciples will betray me.
The son of mankind lives according to Scripture;
It would have been better if the traitor had not been born."

10. Peter waived to John who in turn asked the Lord,
Who [among them] was to betray Him; this He should tell them.
Christ said: "Look at me and take notice,
It is he to whom I give the bread dipped in wine."[55]

11. He dipped the bread in the wine and gave it to Judas:
"What you want to do, do this soon, just as you have it in mind."
He stood up and immediately went away
To the houses of Caiphas and Anna.

12. Now the Son of Man has been explained, and with Him God is explained.
"My beloved sons," He said, "I do not want to conceal from you
That the time is coming when I have to part from you,
And you will experience lamenting and suffering.

13. I'll leave the world and go to my Father
To prepare for you the place where you will join me.
But take heart, do not be too saddened,
Your suffering will turn into joy.

14. I will not leave you as orphans, I'll go and return to you,
Then you will experience extraordinary happiness.
A woman feels pain when she is about to give birth,
But once she has brought to life [the baby], she forgets the pain for her joy.

15. Finally, I'll teach you a new law,
Love each other from the bottom of your heart in full loyalty
As I have loved you in my life,
Even as I am giving my life to you through my death.

16. If you have loved me, keep these words[56] in mind,
And my Father will love you in return.
Whatever you will ask from Him He will grant you
Both here in human life[57] and in eternity.

17. You will all depart from Me and leave Me alone,
But my Father in Heaven will stand by Me after all.
It is written that when the shepherd is struck
Then all the sheep will be chased away as well.

18. You will be angry with Me tonight,
Satan requested the privilege to forcefully press you all through the sifter.

---

[55] Literally: 'wet bite.'
[56] Literally: 'speech.'
[57] Literally: 'in this time.'

I begged for your sake, Simon, that you may hold to your belief,
And once you would be converted, you should be the one to strengthen your
brothers."

19. Then Simon Peter said: "Oh Lord, this shall not happen,
I want to die with You, my most beloved Master!"
The Lord said: "The truth of your words will be proven tonight,[58]
Before the rooster will have crowed, you will have denied me thrice."

20. This, oh God, Your son has suffered for us at the Hour of Vespers.
I beg You on behalf of His suffering, free us from our sins.
Help us to avoid all sins from now on
For which He had been willing to accept such painful suffering.

IX. Marie Cleopha, Countess of Sultz

Marie was the daughter of the first Margrave of Baden-Durlach, Ernst
of Pfortzheim (1482–1553), who ruled from 1533 to 1552, when he vol-
untarily stepped down, probably because of his advanced age. Ernst
married Elisabeth (1494–1518), the daughter of Margrave Frederick of
Brandenburg-Ansbach. Their fifth child was Marie Cleopha (1515–80),
who wed William, Count of Sultz, in 1548. He died in 1566. Marie
composed a number of church songs. Beyond this not much is known
about her.

No. 1: Oh God in the Highest,[59] trustingly I call upon You[60]
(*Ach Gott in deinem Reiche, ich rueff dich trewlich an*)

1. Oh God in the Highest,
Trustingly I am calling upon You,
Just as You told me to do,
Please do not abandon me.[61]
        You told me to carry the cross,
If I wanted to be Your servant.
But now my heart is near despairing
And does not want to submit.

---

[58]   The poet uses the verb "ereugen," meaning 'be revealed to your eyes.'
[59]   Literally: 'in Your kingdom.'
[60]   Quoted from Philipp Wackernagel, ed., *Das deutsche Kirchenlied*, vol. 4, no. 1037.
[61]   Literally: 'You would not want to abandon me.'

2. Grant me, Lord, Your mercy
That I might have the will power
To submit myself
At the Foot of Your cross:
    Create in my heart
The image of Your servant David
Who, likewise, under great pains
Had to be chased away from his son.

3. He was not only chased away from his son,
But also from his best friends
So that he did no longer dare to live freely
In his own house.
    This caused him severe suffering,
It caused him painful woe,
In this misery he began to scream
For You, His God and Lord.

4. He asked You to rescue him
From under his cross,
And said that he wanted
To be patient for Your sake.
    He was willing to suffer
From the people's mockery on Your behalf,
As You had suffered it
Willingly, You loyal God.

5. Wherever I turn
I am despised:
At every place here on Earth
Nothing else counts but violence and money:[62]
    Oh God, I direct my lamentations to You,
I appeal to You trustingly,
Le me not, oh Lord, fall in despair,
Help me with Your grace.

6. With this I entrust
My soul into Your hands:
May You, Lord, bestow upon me
A blessed Christian death:
    As You have promised me
And gave me Your oath

---

[62] Literally: 'violence and luxurious decoration.'

That You would give me
After this [life] eternal happiness.

No. 2: In Sorrow and Pains (*Mit kummer vnd schmertz*)

1. With sorrow and pain
My heart was
Once upon a time[63]
Mortally wounded.
There was no consolation
That could have freed me,
I struggled with death
In fear and misery.
        Despite my complete innocence
I bear patiently
My suffering,
I hope that God will be my helpmate.

2. God, grant me Your grace,
Provide me
With Your divine advice,
As I shout out to You:
Otherwise there is no consolation
That could liberate me
From fear and pain,
Oh You my Creator.
        There is only Your might
Staying forever
In my heart
Which will sustain me in this pain.

3. I cry out to God
Both day and night:
"To You I yell,
Oh Lord, help me,
Stand by me
Through Your son
In whom I have trust
And on whom I rely.
        He keeps me alive
Through His might,
His eternal words.
I build upon them both here and there."

---

[63] Literally: 'in one hour.'

4. Then God blessed me with His grace
And heard what needs I had.
He came to me
And quickly removed
My sorrow and pain,
He gave me His advice,
His divine word,
Was my treasure.
    It filled me with joy
In my pain.
He said to me:
"I have come to offer you help."

5. God's grace is great
Without any limit.[64]
I will announce it in public
For the rest of my life,
That my God
Has listened to me.
For this I thank You,
Oh God, help me
    That I might properly be
Thankful in my heart
For Your Grace
For the rest of my life.[65]

6. My God, preserve,
Through Your might,
My life
Because I belong to You.
In this world
Are set up
So many traps and snares
That I often think
    "How will you survive
In this struggle?
The evil world
Has set up its yarns and nets."

7. Indeed, God's words
Are my treasure
Upon which I trust

---

[64] Literally: 'without any measure.'
[65] The verses nos. 9–12 had to be rearranged to make sense in the English translation.

With full confidence:
My actions and decisions
And everything what I own
I entrust to You,
Oh Lord, help me.
    Do not turn away
In the last hour [of my life]
Oh God, from me.
I entrust my soul and life to You.

8. Rescue me, God,
From the devil's might
When his bitter death
Will strike me.
God, Father, Son
On the highest throne,
God, Holy Spirit,
Grant me Your mercy.
    In the end
Send me Your help,
Do this quickly,
Turn the devil's trickery away from me as soon as possible.

9. After I have lamented for a long time
Finally the last day will arrive
At which we will depart
And turn into dust.
But we have to stand
In front of God's throne,
No wealth can prevent it[66]
Which will be entirely despised.
    The world's favor
Is all for nought.
Oh God, may Your suffering
Be of assistance to us.

X. Klara, Duchess of Pomerania

The hymn book 'A New Christian Book of Psalms . . . ' (*Ein new Christlich Psalmbvch*), printed by Gimel Bergen in Dresden, 1594, contains a selection of church songs not only by Martin Luther, but also by many other male and female poets. One of these is Klara, Duchess of

---

[66] Literally: 'splendor.'

Pomerania (1550–98), who dedicated her hymn to an unknown person only identified by the acronym "A.Z.S.Z."[67]

The song has no specific title; instead it is introduced as "Der Durchleuchtigen Hochgebornen Fürstin vnd F. Frawen Claren gebornen zu Braunschweig vnd Lüneburg, ec. Hertzogin zu Pommern ec. Vorgemels Herren Gemahlin Reim" ('The Rhymes by the High-Born, Illustrious Duchess, Lady Klara, born into the House of Brunswick and Lüneburg, etc., Duchess of Pomerania and wife of the Aforementioned Lord').

1. Everything that God
Has created here on Earth,
Son, moon, all brilliant stars,[68]
All beautiful flowers,
The many kinds of animals,
And also time itself within a year's course,
    Reveals its creator
Through its good order
And freely teaches
That the Almighty truly exists.

2. By its own measure
Grow, bloom, fade, and wither
All leaves and the green grass.
Sun, moon, stars
Are arranged according to an order
None of them gets lost in its course,
    Instead they stand firmly
As their course always has been,
Which certainly demonstrates
The order set up by God.

3. According to His nature
Everything performs forever
In eternity
And according to this reason
All things shall
Be administered
    So that they obediently follow[69]
The obvious order,

---

[67] Quoted by Philipp Wackernagel, ed., *Das deutsche Kirchenlied*, vol. 4, no. 1026.

[68] With 'earth' the poet means the totality of creation, including the stars and the planets.

[69] To make sense out of these first six lines, the translation rests on conjecture and rearrangement of the verses.

And everything will continue
In this way forever.

4. Try to differentiate between the time
Of joy and time of suffering,
If you want to live in peace;
Arrange all things
And bring them to an orderly conclusion
Which will give you a virtuous life.[70]
      Stay pious and continue to pray,
Be quiet, be obedient, speak up when necessary
And trust in God
Who knows how to give help, consolation, and advice.

XI. Conclusion

Further sixteenth-century women poets could be included here as well, but the religious songs or hymns are fairly repetitive, even though inter- pretations might reveal new perspectives or poetic messages, shedding different light on individual songs. Suffice it here to list the names of all those remaining female poets included in my anthology *'Mein Seel fang an zu singen'* but whose poems I have not translated here:

— Anna of Quernheim (before 1520–90)[71]
— Maria, Landgravine of Thuringia and Margravine of Meissen (1515–83)
— Dorothea Susanna, Duchess of Saxony-Weimar (1544–92)
— Countess Anna of the Palatinate (1552–1632)
— Sophie Hedwig, Duchess of Pomerania (1561–1631)
— Margravine of Baden (no first name and no life dates are given, but her poem was published in 1612 in Hamburg)
— Anna, Countess of Stollberg (died in 1620)

For the history of early-modern German women's literature one needs to consider the songbooks created by nuns in various North German convents, even though they were probably not the creators of the songs, but instead copied them from older sources (which in turn could have been created by some female writers, although scholarship traditionally assumes that only men—monks and clerics—could have composed

---

[70] The term 'fromen' carries many different meanings, such as 'profit,' 'virtue,' 'reason,' and 'morality.'

[71] Gertrud Angermann, *Anna von Quernheim (vor 1520–1590). Die erste bekannte Liederdichterin Westfalens und 25 ihrer geistlichen Gesänge in niederdeutscher Sprache* (Bielefeld: Aisthesis-Verlag, 1996).

them): *Wienhäuser Liederbuch* (ca. 1439–69), *Ebstorfer Liederbuch* (end of the fifteenth/early sixteenth century), *Liederbuch der Anna von Köln* (ca. 1500–24), and the *Liederbuch der Catherina Tirs* (1588).[72] The texts of the songs contained in the *Wienhäuser Liederbuch* and the *Ebstorfer Liederbuch*, and in the *Liederbuch der Catherina Tirs* can be found in my *'Mein Seel fang an zu singen'*; the songs collected by Anna of Köln were published by Walter Salmen and Johannes Koepp in 1954.[73]

---

[72] For the relevant bibliographical sources and for historical, literary, and even art-historical background information, see my book *'Mein Seel fang an zu singen'* (2002).

[73] Walter Salmen and Johannes Koepp, *Liederbuch der Anna von Köln (um 1500)*, Denkmäler rheinischer Musik, 4 (Düsseldorf: L. Schwann, 1954).

Interpretive Essay

The Rediscovery of Women's Voices through the Investigation of Hitherto Ignored Sources

Did late-medieval women actually compose love poetry?

With few exceptions medieval courtly love poetry was, perhaps not so surprisingly, dominated by male poets. This has been, by and large, the conclusion drawn by most literary historians until very recently. Although the Old Norwegian and Old Icelandic Skáldonur (tenth and eleventh centuries[1]) and the Old Occitan *troubairitz* (Southern France, or Provence, first half of the twelfth century[2])—both terms signifying women poets—experienced a short period of flowering, their influence did not last for long, and they did not find followers in any other European medieval language as far as modern scholarship has been able to ascertain.[3] Certainly, we often hear female voices, that is, male poets' thinly veiled masks utilized to expand their poetic repertoire, but these poems cannot be identified as contributions by women authors.[4] Maaike Meijer's attempt, for instance, to accept female voices within medieval Dutch dawn songs as evidence for female poetry to some extent ignores the constraints of a literary genre and represents more wishful thinking than historical

---

[1] Sandra B. Straubhaar, "The Forgotten Skáldkonur and their Place in Early Scandinavian Culture," *The Worlds of Medieval Women. Creativity, Influence, Imagination*, ed. Constance H. Berman, Charles W. Connell, and Judith Rice Rothschild (Morgantown: West Virginia University Press, 1985), 14–23; Sandra Ballif Straubhaar, "Skáldkonur," *Medieval Scandinavia. An Encyclopedia*, ed. Phillip Pulsiano (New York and London: Garland, 1993), 594–96.

[2] Angelika Rieger, *Trobairitz. Der Beitrag der Frau in der altokzitanischen höfischen Lyrik. Edition des Gesamtkorpus*, Beihefte zur Zeitschrift für Romanische Philologie, 233 (Tübingen: Niemeyer, 1991).

[3] Peter Dronke, *Women Writers of the Middle Ages. A Critical Study of Texts from Perpetua (†203) to Marguerite Porete (†1310)* (Cambridge: Cambridge University Press, 1984); Straubhaar, "The Forgotten Skáldkonur," 20, reminds us that "[a]s attractive as this depiction of poetry as a lost female art might be, the fact is that for the Viking Age . . . the extant verse suggests that poetry was a male-dominated tradition in which our Group *I skáldkonur* were obliged to display an extraordinary level of poetic skill and/or strength of character for their contributions to be recorded and transmitted."

[4] Anne Lingard Klinck and Ann Marie Rasmussen, eds., *Medieval Woman's Song: Cross-Cultural Approaches*, Middle Ages Series (Philadelphia: University of Pennsylvania Press, 2002).

fact.[5] Quite understandably, Meijer, like many other traditional scholars, commits the fallacy of accepting a fictional female voice within a traditional dialogic genre as a reflection of a literary-historical fact without considering the context and the extenuating social-historical circumstances. Similarly, optimistic claims by feminist scholars such as Susan Boynton that "women performed their own music or adapted the music of others to their own taste and requirements," so far represent mostly fascinating but not sufficiently documented hypotheses and are not supported by textual evidence, unless we accept Boynton's conclusion: "the documented activities of noblewomen and their ladies-in-waiting suggest that they created music and poetry which is lost, or extant but anonymous."[6] It is true, however, that medieval courtly literature contains many intriguing references to professional female musicians and highly trained aristocratic women performing songs and playing musical instruments, such as Isolde in Gottfried of Strassburg's *Tristan*, a jongleur's sister in *Guillaume de Dole*, Nicolette in *Aucassin et Nicolette*, many of the ladies in Boccaccio's *Decameron*, and Tarsia, Apollonius's daughter in the enormously popular *Apollonius of Tyre*.[7] But did noble courtly women also compose poetry, write romances, and create art works? Did they have the education, financial support, and public approval?[8]

---

5   *The Defiant Muse. Dutch and Flemish Feminist Poems from the Middle Ages to the Present. A Bilingual Anthology*, ed. and with an Introduction by Maaike Meijer, co-editors: Erica Eijsker, Ankie Peypers, and Yopie Prins, The Defiant Muse Series (New York: The Feminist Press, 1998), 2–3.

6   Susan Boynton, "Women's Performance of the Lyric before 1500," *Medieval Woman's Song*, ed. Anne Lingard Klinck and Ann Marie Rasmussen, 47–65, here 47 and 59.

7   Joan M. Ferrante, "Beyond the Borders of Nation and Discipline," *The Future of the Middle Ages. Medieval Literature in the 1990s*, ed. William D. Paden (Gainesville et al.: University Press of Florida, 1994), 145–63, here 158–62; Aileen Ann Macdonald, "The Female *Tenso*: Alamanda's Response to Guiraut de Bornelh," *The World and its Rival. Essays on Literary Imagination in Honor of Per Nykrog*, ed. Kathryn Karczewska and Tom Conley, Faux Titre: Etudes de langue et littérature françaises publiées, 172 (Amsterdam and Atlanta: Editions Rodopi, 1999), 79–92, here 87–88; for further examples, see Susan Boynton, "Women's Performance."

8   For a broad, interdisciplinary overview, see Louise O. Vasvári, "Retrieving the Power of Women's Voices in the *Frauenlied*," *Palimpszeszt* 19 (2002), internet journal, see at: http://magyar-irodalom.elte.hu/palimpszeszt/19_szam/index.html. She offers many text examples with English translations, though none in German. For Northern French examples, see *Songs of the Women Trouvères*, ed., trans., and introduced by Eglal Doss-Quinby, Joan Tasker Grimbert, Wendy Pfeffer, Elizabeth Aubrey (New Haven and London: Yale University Press, 2001), 14–26; whereas their documentary evidence is rather slim, with the exception of the guild necrologies for the *Puy d'Arras*, they were able to identify eight named women trouvères: Blanche de Castille, the Dame de Gosnai, the Dame de la Chauci, the Duchesse de Lorraine, Lorete, Dame Margot, Maroie de Diergnau, and Sainte des Prez, 26–32.

Fortunately, as the present volume indicates, we might be closer to uncovering hitherto unknown female voices from the German Middle Ages than was previously thought possible, though our focus rests on the fifteenth and sixteenth centuries. The poetic texts translated here apparently represent a lost or at least hidden tradition and remind us of the critical problems of research in the history of women's literature, since we know still far too little to formulate absolute and comprehensive statements about women's actual contributions.[9] On the one hand, the religious songs, introduced here, clearly demonstrate that women were actively involved in the creation of lyric poetry, at least during the sixteenth century. Most of these texts are unequivocally identified by a name and can be attributed to specific, well-known women poets. But often even a careful analysis will not easily allow us to identify in a concrete manner particularly female concerns, issues, or themes in these church songs or songs for private meditation. The anonymous secular women's songs, on the other hand, represent a much more thorny issue, as we have to rely on fairly tenuous external circumstances and the textual content to strengthen the claim that they were composed by women.

Several factors, however, deserve to be considered right from the beginning as they support the overall notion of female literacy during the German late Middle Ages: 1. a significant and large number of women were active as scribes (Clara Hätzlerin) and patrons (Ottilia Fenchlerin);[10] 2. the interest in women's songs was not limited to a female audience; 3. most of the songs translated here fall into the category of "popular poetry" and were mostly disregarded by traditional scholarship until recently because of their allegedly mediocre literary quality.[11] These factors are the more surprising since feminist-oriented

---

[9] Sheila Fisher and Janet E. Halley, eds., *Seeking the Woman in Late Medieval Literature: Essays in Feminist Contextual Criticism* (Knoxville: University of Tennessee Press, 1989); Bonnie S. Anderson and Judith P. Zinnser, *A History of Their Own: Women in Europe from Prehistory to the Present*, 2nd rev. ed. (1988; New York and Oxford: Oxford University Press, 2000).

[10] Alison I. Beach, *Women as Scribes. Book Production and Monastic Reform in Twelfth-Century Bavaria*, Cambridge Studies in Paleography and Codicology, 9 (Cambridge: Cambridge University Press, 2002), demonstrates that during the Renaissance of the twelfth century many convent women were already active as scribes.

[11] For the complex issue of elite versus popular poetry or song, see Albert Wellek, "Renaissance- und Barock-Synästhesie. Die Geschichte des Doppelempfindens im 16. und 17. Jahrhundert," *Deutsche Vierteljahresschrift für Literaturwissenschaft und Geistesgeschichte* 9 (1931): 534–84; Wolfgang Wiora, *Das deutsche Lied. Zur Geschichte und Ästhetik einer musikalischen Gattung* (Wolfenbüttel and Zürich: Möseler, 1971); for non-German evidence regarding women's contributions, see Maria Coldwell, "*Jougleresses* and *Troubairitz*: Secular Musicians in Medieval France," *Women Making Music: The Western Art Tradition, 1150–1950*, ed. Jane Bowers and Judith Tick

scholarship has made great advances over the last ten to fifteen years, as Jocelyn Wogan-Browne has reminded us through her recent research report, but she would have been well advised to consult these late-medieval literary sources as well.[12]

The history of late-medieval and early-modern popular poetry

Why have most of these songs, which either strongly suggest female authorship or are clearly identifiable as such, been ignored by modern research? What kind of songs are we dealing with, and how are we to evaluate their literary quality? In other words, why do they not yet figure within the literary canon? Do they actually support the claim that women held a noteworthy stake in the history of late-medieval and early-modern German literature? If scholarship has mostly disregarded them until now, what would justify their integration into our current canon now? The standard, though somewhat outdated, literary history by Hans Rupprich, for instance, briefly touches upon the genre of popular poetry as a cumulative corpus, but the author only takes a more thorough look at the historical songs and ballads within this genre ("historisch-politische[s] Lied") because they allow him to discuss the political and military background in specific terms. He also mentions love songs, but only because here he discovers evidence that this poetic genre broadly reflected the ordinary person's concerns and interests.[13] Gender issues, however, never play a role in his investigations of these popular songs. Wolfgang Suppan, a major authority on German "Volkslieder," identifies, following Heinrich Kramm's sociological

(Urbana: University of Illinois Press, 1986), 43–44; Walter Salmen, *Spielfrauen im Mittelalter* (Hildesheim: Georg Olms, 2000).

[12] Jocelyn Wogan-Browne, "Analytical Survey 5: 'Reading is Good Prayer': Recent Research on Female Reading Communities," *New Medieval Literatures*, Vol. 5, ed. Rita Copeland, David Lawton, and Wendy Scase (Oxford: Oxford University Press, 2002), 229–97; see also Albrecht Classen and Peter Dinzelbacher, "Weltliche Literatur von Frauen des Mittelalters. Bemerkungen zur jüngeren Forschung," *Mediaevistik* 8 (1995): 55–73.

[13] Hans Rupprich, *Die deutsche Literatur vom späten Mittelalter bis zum Barock*, 2nd Part: *Das Zeitalter der Reformation 1520–1570*, Geschichte der deutschen Literatur von den Anfängen bis zur Gegenwart, 4/2 (Munich: Beck, 1973), 232–40; Peter Nusser, *Deutsche Literatur im Mittelalter. Lebensformen, Wertvorstellungen und literarische Entwicklungen*, Kröners Taschenausgabe, 480 (Stuttgart: Kröner, 1992), 364–72, erroneously argues that most of these popular songs were composed by members of the rural population—entirely disregarding all modern research on "Volkslieder." Despite occasional attempts to explore new avenues in the area of late-medieval song poetry, the current research does not basically go beyond Rupprich's observations: see, for instance, *Lied im deutchen Mittelalter. Überlieferung, Typen, Gebrauch. Chiemsee-Colloquium 1991*, ed. Cyril Edwards, Ernst Hellgardt, and Norbert H. Ott (Tübingen: Niemeyer, 1996); see, however, the comprehensive survey in my *Deutsche Liederbücher des 15. und 16. Jahrhunderts*, Volksliedstudien, 1 (Münster, New York et al.: Waxmann, 2001).

analysis, the following groups as authors of these popular songs: lawyers, clerics, Latin teachers, academically-trained medical doctors and students, merchants, book printers, apothecaries, scribes, administrators, custos (church guardians), and other members of the upper and lower intelligentsia.[14] Women, of course, do not represent a separate social class, but Suppan never even considers the possibility of female authorship outside of his male-dominated rubrics.[15]

We are obviously faced by several major research problems. On the one hand, all of our songs were composed during the fifteenth and sixteenth centuries. Although both centuries have increasingly become the object of thorough scholarly investigations,[16] lyric poetry from that period does not enjoy much interest, especially if it is not primarily concerned with the Protestant Reformation.[17] The major reason seems to be that traditionally medieval scholarship has focused almost exclusively on twelfth- and thirteenth-century courtly love poetry (*Minnesang*) and also on some of its late-medieval successors, such as Neidhard, Steinmar, Johannes Hadloub, Hugo of Montfort, and Oswald of Wolkenstein, to the disadvantage of late fifteenth- and sixteenth-century poetry.[18] On the other hand, most of the popular songs have been

---

[14] Wolfgang Suppan, *Deutsches Liedleben zwischen Renaissance und Barock. Die Schichtung des deutschen Liedgutes in der zweiten Hälfte des 16. Jahrhunderts*, Mainzer Studien zur Musikwissenschaft, 4 (Tutzing: Hans Schneider, 1973), 37–38; Heinrich Kramm, "Besitz- und Bildungsschichten der mitteldeutschen Städte im 16. Jahrhundert," *Vierteljahresschrift für Sozial- und Wirtschaftsgeschichte* 51 (1964): 454–91.

[15] For a broad criticism of patriarchal literary history, see Ria Lemaire, "Rethinking Literary History," *Historiography of Women's Cultural Traditions*, ed. Maaike Meijer and Jetty Schaap (Dordrecht, Holland, and Providence, RI: Foris Publications, 1987), 180–93.

[16] See, for example, the journals *Fifteenth-Century Studies* and *Sixteenth-Century Studies*.

[17] The exceptions would be religious poetry reflecting the Protestant Reformation and the attempts by the Catholic Church to regain its status during the Counter-Reformation, and poetry composed by the *Meistersinger*—urban craftsmen who organized themselves in singing schools: see Hans-Georg Kemper, *Deutsche Lyrik der frühen Neuzeit*, Vol. 1: *Epochen- und Gattungsprobleme. Reformationszeit* (Tübingen: Niemeyer, 1987); Herbert Walz, *Deutsche Literatur der Reformationszeit. Eine Einführung*, Germanistische Einführungen (Darmstadt: Wissenschaftliche Buchgesellschaft, 1988), 30–61; a major survey was presented in *Repertorium der Sangsprüche und Meisterlieder des 12. bis 18. Jahrhunderts*, ed. Horst Brunner and Burghart Wachinger, 16 vols. (Tübingen: Niemeyer, 1986–96).

[18] As modern research has realized, late-medieval and early-modern secular love poetry experienced a tremendous transformation and absolutely deserves to be studied as a separate subject of its own; for a still relevant overview, see Olive Sayce, *The Medieval German Lyric 1150–1300. The Development of its Themes and Forms in their European Context* (Oxford: At the Clarendon Press, 1982); Marion E. Gibbs and Sidney M. Johnson, *Medieval German Literature. A Companion* (New York and London: Garland, 1997), 279–303; Wolfgang Suppan, *Deutsches Liedleben*, 55–75, et passim; Burghart Wachinger, "Liebe und Literatur im spätmittelalterlichen Schwaben und Franken. Zur Augsburger Sammelhandschrift der Clara Hätzlerin," *Deutsche Vierteljahresschrift für Literaturwissenschaft und*

preserved in so-called "Liederbücher," or songbooks, which combine a wide range of lyrical genres with a considerable mass appeal. As a consequence, many Germanist scholars have disregarded them as literary material unworthy of their attention.[19] Some of these songbooks were still kept in manuscript form, others were collections of individual broadsheets, reflecting the new role played by the printing press invented around 1450.[20] A large percentage of these songs, whether by male or female poets, were recorded many times in different formats, then were printed and reprinted, and many of them appear to have been composed by representatives of various social classes. In other words, since the fifteenth century lyric poetry underwent a tremendous democratization process involving not only urban craftsmen, but also miners, soldiers, students, merchants, and other professions. Suddenly we are faced with the phenomenon of "popular" poetry and culture, and Germanists and musicologists have mostly distanced themselves from both. Nevertheless, many poets still belonged to the aristocracy and considered their compositions to be reflections of their own class and social status.[21] Most of the songbooks were the work of aristocratic or urban intellectuals, some of them were copied down by professional scribes, and those produced in the sixteenth century were the result of collectors who put together a large number of individual broadsheets for archival reasons.[22]

When the Romantics discovered this popular poetry at the turn of the eighteenth century, they quickly assumed that these songs had somehow mysteriously grown out of the people's soul during the early history of Germany, hence "Volkslieder"—songs of the people. Johann Gottfried Herder, Achim von Arnim, and Clemens von Brentano began with a major collection process, and the latter two published the famous anthology *Des Knaben Wunderhorn* (1805–08). Their efforts

Geistesgeschichte 56, 3 (1982): 386–406. To remedy the problematic situation, I have recently investigated the contination of the dawn-song tradition: "Das deutsche Tagelied in seinen spätmittelalterlichen und frühneuzeitlichen Varianten," *Etudes Germaniques* 54, 2 (1999): 173–96.

[19] Albrecht Classen, "Die historische Entwicklung eines literarischen Sammlungstypus. Das Liederbuch vom 14. bis zum 17. Jahrhundert—von der *Weingartner Liederhandschrift* bis zum *Venus Gärtlein*," "*daß gepfleget werde der feste Buchstab*". *Festschrift für Heinz Rölleke zum 65. Geburtstag am 6. November 2001*, ed. Lothar Bluhm and Achim Hölter (Trier: Wissenschaftlicher Verlag, 2001), 26–40.

[20] Uwe Neddermeyer, *Von der Handschrift zum gedruckten Buch. Schriftlichkeit und Leseinteresse im Mittelalter und in der frühen Neuzeit. Quantitative und qualitative Aspekte*, 2 vols., Buchwissenschaftliche Beiträge aus dem deutschen Bucharchiv München, 61 (Wiesbaden: Harrassowitz, 1998).

[21] Wolfgang Suppan, *Deutsches Liedleben*, 11–17, 37–41.

[22] Albrecht Classen, *Deutsche Liederbücher*, 8–25.

subsequently led to much more serious and comprehensive studies and anthologies by nineteenth-century scholars such as Franz M. Böhme, Franz Wilhelm Freiherr von Ditfurth, Friedrich Karl Freiherr von Erlach, Ludwig Erk, Karl Goedeke, Arthur Kopp, Rochus von Liliencron, Julius Tittmann, Ludwig Tobler, and Ludwig Uhland.[23]

Modern scholarship dedicated to the "Volkslied" has considerably changed since then, as documented, for instance, by eighty-eight years of research at the Deutsches Volksliedarchiv in Freiburg i.Br., founded by John Meyer on May 2, 1914,[24] which also publishes the *Jahrbuch für Volksliedforschung*. But many questions about this vast genre remain unanswered and will require intensive research in the future before we can fully claim to have thoroughly grasped the essence of late-medieval and early-modern popular poetry. The traditional term "Volkslied" can no longer be fully used as appropriate in scholarly discourse, as it implies a deeply Romantic notion of this genre. This notion has nothing in common with literary-historical reality—but for lack of any other term with the same historical background, I am continuing to use it here, keeping in mind its speculative and maybe even misleading implications.[25] Interestingly, the historical sources never even mention this term, instead they titled their songs employing terms such as "Graßliedlin" (grass or meadow song), "Gassenhawerlin" (popular street song), "Reutererliedlin" (horseman's song), "Bergkreyen" (mountain dance song, or miner's song), "hüpsch new Lied" (beautiful new song), "Gesellenlied" (journeyman's song), and "Straßenlied" (street song). All these terms point to the simple people from the lower classes who seem to have been the creators of this poetry. In reality, however, in most cases their origins can be traced back to an elite culture, both aristocratic and intellectual. Nevertheless, the vast dissemination process, strongly supported by the printing press, erroneously implies the opposite, as if these were songs by and for the people on the street, in the cities, and in the country.

[23] Rolf Wilhelm Brednich, *Die Liedpublizistik im Flugblatt des 15. bis 17. Jahrhunderts*, 2 vols. (Baden-Baden: Koerner, 1974); ibid., Lutz Röhrich, and Wolfgang Suppan, eds., *Handbuch des Volksliedes*, 2 vols. (Munich: Fink, 1973–75); Karina Kellermann, *Abschied vom 'historischen Volkslied': Studien zu Funktion, Ästhetik und Publizität der Gattung historisch-politische Ereignisdichtung*, Hermaea, Neue Folge, 90 (Tübingen: Niemeyer, 2000).

[24] *"Freut euch des Lebens . . ."*. *75 Jahre Deutsches Volksliedarchiv* (Freiburg i.Br.: Deutsches Volksliedarchiv, 1989).

[25] See the criticism by Sonja Kerth, *"Der landsfrid ist zerbrochen". Das Bild des Krieges in den politischen Ereignisdichtungen des 13. bis 16. Jahrhunderts*, Imagines medii aevi, 1 (Wiesbaden: Reichert, 1997); Karina Kellermann, *Abschied vom 'historischen Volkslied'*.

The critical evaluation of late-medieval German "Volkslieder" (plural) has also been severely hampered by a significant quantitative factor; the sheer volume of these popular songs has made it difficult to categorize, comprehend, compare, and examine individual representatives of this expansive genre. A number of important inroads, however, have been undertaken over the last fifteen years or so. Beate Rattay (1986) and Karina Kellermann (2000), for instance, have explored the genre of historical folk songs and impressively profiled, each in her own way, the ideological, social-political, and ethical-moral intentions and directions in these texts.[26] Bertrand Michael Buchmann attempted to analyze these popular songs as literary sources for the medieval and early-modern mental history.[27] Martina Probst uncovered the tradition of spiritual dawn songs among these "Volkslieder";[28] Gaby Herchert studied the erotic imagery and themes in this genre;[29] and Susanne Fritsch-Staar focused on the motif of the mistreated and unhappily married wife in medieval and early-modern songs.[30] To provide an overview and to develop decisive analytic categories to facilitate a better understanding of the historical "Volkslied," I have recently studied twenty major fifteenth- and sixteenth-century songbooks, many of which contain several hundred songs or song-texts.[31]

Mostly, modern opinions about these 'popular songs' were negative because many songs seem to follow the same thematic orientation as the

[26]   Beate Rattay, *Entstehung und Rezeption politischer Lyrik im 15. und 16. Jahrhundert. Die Lieder im Chronicon Helveticum von Aegidius Tschudi*, Göppinger Arbeiten zur Germanistik, 405 (Göppingen: Kümmerle, 1986); Karina Kellermann, *Abschied vom 'historischen Volkslied'*.

[27]   Bertrand Michael Buchmann, *Daz jemant singet oder sait . . . Das volkstümliche Lied als Quelle zur Mentalitätsgeschichte* (Frankfurt a.M., Berlin et al.: Peter Lang, 1995); for a review, see Albrecht Classen, *Jahrbuch für Volksliedforschung* 41 (1996): 115–16.

[28]   Martina Probst, *Nu wache ûf, sünder træge. Geistliche Tagelieder des 13. bis 16. Jahrhunderts. Analysen und Begriffsbestimmung*, Regensburger Beiträge zur deutschen Sprach- und Literaturwissenschaft, Reihe B/Untersuchungen, 17 (Frankfurt a.M., Berlin et al.: Peter Lang, 1999); for a review, see Albrecht Classen, *Jahrbuch für Volksliedforschung* 45 (2001): 296–97.

[29]   Gaby Herchert, *"Acker mir mein bestes Feld". Untersuchungen zu erotischen Liederbuchliedern des späten Mittelalters. Mit Wörterbuch und Textsammlung* (Münster and New York: Waxmann, 1995); for a review, see Albrecht Classen, *Jahrbuch für Volksliedforschung* 43 (1998): 162–64.

[30]   Susanne Fritsch-Staar, *Unglückliche Ehefrauen. Zum deutschsprachigen malmariée-Lied*, Philologische Studien und Quellen, 134 (Berlin: Schmidt, 1995); for a review, see Albrecht Classen, *Jahrbuch für Volksliedforschung* 41 (1996): 125–26.

[31]   Albrecht Classen, *Deutsche Liederbücher des 15. und 16. Jahrhunderts*, Volkslied Studien, 1 (Münster, New York, Munich, and Berlin: Waxmann, 2001); I could have included many more songbooks in my investigation, but I believe that my selection includes the most representative *Liederbücher*. Many songbooks are yet unedited and continue to rest in the various archives in Germany, Switzerland, and Austria, and probably also elsewhere.

courtly love poetry (*Minnesang*); they do not offer significant innovation in style, imagery, or language, and do not reflect truly creative features in contrast to the works of outstanding contemporary poets such as Oswald of Wolkenstein (1376/77–1445), Hans Rosenplüt (ca. 1400/05–ca. 1460), and Michel Beheim (1416–ca. 1475). Max Wehrli curtly summarized the *opinio communis*: "The popular song was created by and for the lay people, and it is predominantly a secular song to be sung as communal entertainment."[32]

Several major themes in "Volkslieder" can be easily identified: a. the vast complex of love, sex, marriage, pregnancy, divorce, and violence; b. historical events; c. religion; d. riddles, jokes, and lies; e. dance and drinking songs; f. war songs (closely related to 'historical events'); g. hunting; h. professional activities such as mining and agriculture; i. children.[33] Whereas courtly love poetry was primarily situated in the world of aristocratic ladies and knights, the "Volkslied" only reiterates, as Wehrli comments, the same themes and motifs, but develops them within the urban and rural context: "The courtly lady is transformed into the 'sweet, sun-tanned girl,' the peasant world is automatically woven into the song's content."[34]

Although most of these popular songs have come down to us anonymously, scholars such as Wolfgang Suppan, Hans Rupprich, Max Wehrli, and Peter Nusser have naively assumed that all poets were male. This traditional and rather unreflected attitude has been firmly cemented in reference works, encyclopedias, and handbooks on the history of German literature.[35] However, as our selection of secular love poetry indicates, rather the opposite appears to have been the case, although we need to examine each case carefully before we can reach definite conclusions.

Neither Elisabeth Borchers nor Marcel Reich-Ranicki live up to the expectations raised by the titles of their anthologies of German women's literature which suggest that a continuous history of female writing from the high Middle Ages to the present can be documented.

---

[32] Max Wehrli, *Geschichte der deutschen Literatur im Mittelalter. Von den Anfängen bis zum Ende des 16. Jahrhunderts*, 3rd, expanded, ed. (1980; Stuttgart: Reclam, 1997), 1073.
[33] Lutz Röhrich, "Die Textgattungen des populären Liedes," *Handbuch des Volksliedes*, vol. 1 (1973), 19–35. (See note 23)
[34] M. Wehrli, *Geschichte der deutschen Literatur*, 1077.
[35] Among the many examples, see *Metzler Literatur Lexikon. Begriffe und Definitionen*, ed. Günther and Irmgard Schweikle, 2nd rev. ed. (Stuttgart: Metzler, 1990), 492f.; only rarely do we find information about the genre in non-German scholarship: see Albrecht Classen, "Late Middle High German, Renaissance, and Reformation," *A Concise History of German Literature to 1900*, ed. Kim Vivian, Studies in German Literature, Linguistics, and Culture (Columbia, SC: Camden House, 1992), 58–90, here 78–79.

Each of these two editors includes a few texts written by mystical visionaries such as Hildegard of Bingen and Mechthild of Magdeburg, or a poem by an anonymous nun from the late twelfth century, but then they jump far into the seventeenth and eighteenth centuries.[36] An earlier attempt by Susan L. Cocalis to trace a continuous history of German feminist poems from the Middle Ages to the present also fell short of its anticipated goals as she includes only two poems by the mystical writer Mechthild of Magdeburg, and then quickly moves into the sixteenth century (Argula of Grumbach).[37] By contrast, the considerable corpus of fifteenth- and sixteenth-century popular women's poetry presented here promises finally to close this gap and to open our eyes to a surprisingly large number of active women writers during this period.

The female voice in late-medieval and early-modern popular poetry

Let us consider some examples in our selection to probe the crucial question of how far we can support our claim of female authorship. Unfortunately, the situation is far from being as clear-cut as we would like it to be, and we need to question all our own assumptions before we proceed further in our investigations. The very first song, Ambras No. XXXVI, *HErtz einiges lieb, dich nicht betrüb*, here no. 1, does nothing more than to formulate expressions of sorrow, obviously because of the separation experienced by the two lovers. According to the statement in the very last line, a young woman—she identifies herself as a virgin—composed the song, and if we can believe this claim, the entire song implies that she sends words of encouragement and love to her boyfriend. She appeals to him to trust in her loyalty and to hold out against society's criticism and opposition to their love relationship. The female singer seems to be strong enough to instill confidence in him as she acknowledges the public pressure exerted on them both, but she states firmly that love can never be maintained without the experience of occasional misfortune and even misery. More important, she

---

[36] *Gedichte von Hildegard von Bingen bis Ingeborg Bachmann*, ed. Elisabeth Borchers (Frankfurt a.M.: Insel, 1987); *Frauen dichten anders. 181 Gedichte. Mit Interpretationen*, ed. Marcel Reich-Ranicki (Frankfurt a.M. and Leipzig: Insel, 1998). My own research has led me to publish an academic anthology incorporating my findings: *Frauen in der deutschen Literaturgeschichte. Die ersten 800 Jahre. Ein Lesebuch*, selection, translation and commentary by Albrecht Classen, Women in German Literature, 4 (New York: Peter Lang, 2000).

[37] *The Defiant Muse. German Feminist Poems from the Middle Ages to the Present. A Bilingual Anthology*, ed. and with an Introduction by Susan L. Cocalis, The Defiant Muse (New York: The Feminist Press, 1986), 2–8.

presents herself as a model for proper behavior, stoic and calm amidst the storm, since her love will remain steadfast and solid for the rest of her life. True love will carry them both through all their trials and tribulations, as it is characterized by profound loyalty. Finally, the narrator confirms that a woman composed this song. The tone of voice, the selection of words and imagery, and a number of internal, yet not verifiable references to a woman's concern, suggest a female poet, especially in the light of the statement in the very last line. Of course, the nagging question remains: Would it not have been possible for a male poet to hide his gender identity so well as to leave the interpreter in limbo? The voluminous collections of late-medieval popular songs contain many examples of anonymous poetry with no possibility of a precise gender attribution. Therefore we need to turn to other, more solid criteria to reach firm ground for our discussion.

The testimony of a fairly large corpus of medieval women's songs, definitely composed by male writers from the high Middle Ages, such as Dietmar von Aist, Walther von der Vogelweide, Neidhart, Otto of Botenlouben, Raimbaut d'Orange, and Raimbaut de Vaqueiras, demonstrates that they always clearly leave markers that allow us to lift the veil and understand the masquerade or the dramatic impetus of separate voices.[38] Perhaps we should distance ourselves from all efforts to search for the actual author of lyric poetry, and simply focus, following Pierre Bec's lead, on its "textual femininity."[39] That would have the advantage of removing all further trouble with the complex ambiguity of our textual source, but would also deprive us of important interpretive tools to gain a deeper understanding of an individual text. Nevertheless, the last line of our poem clearly states: 'It was composed by a beautiful virgin.' Why should we doubt it? There is no obvious reason to take that route, especially as the poetic voice does not reveal any kind of irony and does not express any hidden agenda to ridicule female desire for love. The dearth of external evidence, in remarkable contrast to most of those women's songs which can be clearly attributed to male poets, suggests that "HErtz einiges lieb, dich nicht betrüb" was indeed composed by a female poet, even if final proof escapes us.

---

[38] *Frauenlieder des Mittelalters. Zweisprachig*, trans. and ed. Ingrid Kasten (Stuttgart: Reclam, 1990); see also the introduction by Anne L. Klinck to *Medieval Woman's Song*, ed. Anne Lingard Klinck and Ann Marie Rasmussen, 1–14.

[39] Pierre Bec, "*Trobairitz* et chansons de femme: Contribution à la connaissance du lyrisme féminin au moyen âge," *Cahiers de civilisation médiévale* 22, 3 (1979): 235–62, here 235–36; see also Matilda Tomaryn Bruckner, "Fictions of the Female Voice. The Women Troubadours," *Medieval Woman's Song*, ed. Anne Lingard Klinck and Ann Marie Rasmussen, 127–51, here 134.

The *Ambras* songbook does not contain any hint about the actual person hiding behind the phrase 'beautiful virgin.' Consequently, considering the considerable pressure by male-dominated society on late-medieval women to submit to patriarchal rule,[40] the deliberate formulation of a female perspective and the revelation of a strong female consciousness support the claim of female authorship in this case. Another way to gain additional confirmation might be to compare the women's songs from our selection with those undoubtedly composed by twelfth-century *troubairitz* poems, that is, songs by female aristocrats living in the South of France, the Provence, during the first half of the twelfth century. Those songs, for instance, which are contained in Ottilia Fenchlerin's songbook, offer surprising parallels both in tone and content, which strongly suggests that here we are, indeed, dealing with authentic women's songs.[41] A counter-argument might be that the male poet hiding behind the mask of anonymity had simply learned how to express himself in the vein of a woman and tried to appeal directly to his female audience or to his female patron. However, in practically all cases of women's songs composed by male poets throughout the Middle Ages we easily come across some clues that allow us to identify the composer and his playful intentions.[42] As Ingrid Kasten confirms with respect to Reinmar der Alte (died before 1210):

> the representation of women in Reinmar's woman's song diverges from the representations of women in his men's song, while the portrayal of men in both is consistent. In both types of poetry men typically appear in ideal exemplarity as exceptional singers and as humble men, loyal to the point of self-sacrifice.

---

[40] Lyndal Roper, *The Holy Household. Women and Morals in Reformation Augsburg*, Oxford Studies in Social History (Oxford: Clarendon Press, 1989); for a different perspective, see Heide Wunder, *"Er ist die Sonn', sie ist der Mond". Frauen in der Frühen Neuzeit* (Munich: Beck, 1992). For a study on patriarchy, see Kathy E. Ferguson, "Patriarchy," *Women's Studies Encyclopedia*, Vol. 1: *Views from the Sciences*, ed. Helen Tierney (New York, Westport, CT, and London: Greenwood Press, 1989), 265–67.

[41] Albrecht Classen, "Ottilia Fenchlerin's Songbook: A Contribution to the History of Sixteenth-Century German Women's Literature," *Women in German Yearbook* 14 (1999): 19–40, here 31–32.

[42] This issue is also discussed in *Songs of the Women Trouvères*, ed. Eglal Doss-Quinby et al., 7–14, where Joan Tasker Grimbert emphasizes, 14: "Because there is evidence that European women were indeed composing songs in the high Middle Ages as in earlier periods, by what logic does it follow that none of the extant anonymous chansons de femme were composed by women . . . But if we are content to reduce the many female voices in the chansons de femme to the status of féminité textuelle alone, we run the risk of denying women a place in the pantheon of medieval lyric poetry." There is, however, no absolute logic that would force us to accept this claim, unless we can identify actual texts composed by women. This is, fortunately, the case in *Songs of the Women Trouvères*, and, as I hope to have demonstrated, in the present volume as well.

In contrast, Reinmar's woman's song not only contradicts the image of the indifferent minnelady but goes farther, portraying the loving woman as a person who does not understand what is happening to her and who is basically incapable of resisting the man's will.[43]

The song in Ambras (no. LXV): *ACh mutter liebste mutter mein*, here no. 3, very much leans in this direction, as the staging of a female voice specifically for male interests is quite obvious. Although the singer is a goldsmith's daughter, we cannot confirm at all whether she composed this song as well. Instead, we only learn that she performed this song once again. Clear preference is given to students as the most worthy lovers, and the song strongly implies that young women should disregard their mothers' advice and choose students as lovers who are characterized as being much more attractive than the boring and alcoholic merchants.[44] It seems highly likely that the original author was a (male) student himself who was familiar with the tradition of women's songs and here developed it further to project himself and his fellows as erotically highly attractive to women.

The situation seems to be slightly different in Ambras No. CIX: *ACh Gott wem sol ichs klagen*, here no. 4, as a true female voice emerges, but a careful reading immediately indicates that the song is situated in the tradition of anti-Catholic sentiments during the early Reformation when Martin Luther and his fellow Protestants ridiculed and seriously challenged the institution of a convent and adamantly fought to abolish it altogether, promoting the idea of all women marrying, forcing them to return to the family.[45] So the woman's voice might easily have been a propagandistic ploy to support the case against the institution of the monastery and to idealize marriage for all women. On the other hand, we also know of actual women writers who had left a convent, such as Florentina of Oberweimar, and publicly spoke up against the practice of forcefully placing young girls in convents without considering their own interests and wishes.[46]

---

[43]   Ingrid Kasten, "The Conception of Female Roles in the Woman's Song of Reinmar and the Comtessa de Dia," *Medieval Woman's Song*, ed. Anne Lingard Klinck and Ann Marie Rasmussen, 152–67, here 159.

[44]   Ann Marie Rasmussen, *Mothers and Daughters* in Medieval German Literature (Syracuse, NY: Syracuse University Press, 1997), 163–88, refers to additional songs in this tradition and critically analyzes the male perspective hidden therein.

[45]   Susan C. Karant-Nunn, "Reformation Society, Women and the Family," *The Reformation World*, ed. Andrew Pettegree (London and New York: Routledge, 2000), 433–60; Richard Marius, *Martin Luther. The Christian between God and Death* (Cambridge, MA, and London: The Belknap Press of Harvard University Press, 1999), 310–14.

[46]   Albrecht Classen, "Frauen in der deutschen Reformation: Neufunde von Texten und Autorinnen sowie deren Neubewertung", *Die Frau in der Renaissance*, ed. Paul Gerhard Schmidt. Wolfenbütteler Abhandlungen zur Renaissanceforschung, 14 (Wiesbaden: Harrassowitz,

With Heidelberg no. 83: *Ach Gott, ich klag dir meine nott* we begin to tread on more solid ground, as the female voice, who does not identify herself more specifically, aggressively attacks her former lover who has abandoned her, betraying her trust and loyalty, and has taken another lover. The first two lines of the third stanza are so strong in their aggressive criticism that it seems unlikely that a male voice would have resorted to the disguise of a female voice: 'What good will your false trickery do to you, lad, / as you are such a disloyal person!' Consequently the singer sets up a clear barrier between herself and her former lover whom she never wants to see again, as we hear in the fourth stanza: 'go away, go away . . . / you are expelled from my heart, yes, from my heart.' Moreover, she warns all other young women to be more circumspect and to protect themselves against deceptive young men who only want to enjoy a sexual relationship with them but have no intention of developing a loyal and trustworthy partnership. As the last two lines of stanza five indicate, the female singer reflects a deep-seated distrust of all men because of their pattern of betrayal, and she uses her song as a public platform to attack the other gender for its lack of honesty and constancy: 'You men are always true to your kind, / weeds do not disappear from the garden.'[47]

This theme finds remarkable parallels in contemporary European women's love poetry, such as by Isabella Whitney and Catherine des Roches of whom we know for sure that they actually composed their lyric poetry.[48] Insofar as our anonymous poet specifically addresses her personal suffering and the trauma she had to undergo in the breakup of her love relationship, it only makes sense to identify her as a woman who voiced her bitterness and frustration, and launched a public attack against her unfaithful lover.

As the poet in Ottilia No. III *Freündliches herz*, here no. 1, indicates, the loss of the male lover could represent a severe shock and was feared

---

1994), 188–89. Luther's own wife, Katharina von Bora, had been a nun in the Nimbschen convent near Grimma, from which she had escaped in 1523. She married Luther on June 13, 1525; for more details on Katharina, see http://www.bautz.de/ bbkl/k/ Katharina_v_b.shtml

[47] Perhaps this would be the "feminist" attribute discussed by Susan L. Cocalis, *The Defiant Muse. German Feminist Poems*, xv. For her the term implies "nuances, or thematic or formal aberrations from traditional norms, or lapses that suggest a new consciousness of the poet's situation as a woman, and specifically, as a woman writer. Thematically, this aberration can be found in a woman's defense of her writing; in the way that she approaches themes beyond the allegedly female domains of love, sentiment, religion, and the family; in her attempt to redefine herself, her relationship to men, her sexuality, or her role in society; in her anger or resentment at her 'lot in life'; and in the way she feels alienated or displaced from the traditionally female sphere."

[48] Ann Rosalind Jones, *The Currency of Eros. Women's Love Lyric in Europe, 1540–1620*, Women of Letters (Bloomington and Indianapolis: Indiana University Press, 1990), 43–78.

by many women with great trepidation. The poetic discourse obviously allowed for significant compensation and the recollection of spiritual strength. The first lines in the second stanza confirm how much she is afraid of losing him and that she uses the song as a means to regain the young man's love:

> Friendly image
> > display your grace
> toward your poor woman servant,
> when you want to, it can get lost,
> take me into your arms
> > full with joy
> > snuggled to your chest,
> your arms hold me tightly.

Can we, however, trust poetic expressions of profound emotional experiences, such as in Ottilia No. XX *Kein lieberer auf erdt war nie geboren*, here no. 4? Does this poem reflect truly female experiences, or could a male poet also have developed such images of a suffering woman who laments the painful separation from her lover? There is no name at the end of the poem, and the narrative voice does not specify his/her identity, although the entire framework strongly suggests that the singer is female. Would a male poet have felt comfortable employing the mask of a woman to develop such passionate expressions? It seems unlikely, but it is not impossible either, although the singer emphasizes at the end: 'if I cannot gain your love, / I will die from suffering.' Ottilia No. XXIII *Gross lust hab ich zu singen gehabt*, here no. 4, provides more intriguing evidence, as the female voice emphasizes her activity as a poet and that the song serves her as medium to convey her love to her boyfriend. Her wishes indicate her desire to marry, as she hopes to join his family soon: 'Oh, if everything went my way / your mother would have to be my mother-in-law.' Even though the poem never fully becomes autobiographical and always stays within the world of lyrical fiction, some of the concluding verses appear to reflect a confessional mode. In fact, the song seems to have been originally destined for a poetry album in which the female author intended to relate to her boyfriend how much she loved him, that she was thinking of him all the time, and utilized the written text as a means to illustrate her deep passion for him:[49]

---

[49] An almost perfect example for this phenomenon would be *Die Darnfelder Liederhandschrift 1546–1565*, based on initial work by Arthur Hübner and Ada-Elise Beckmann, ed. Rolf Wilhelm Brednich, Schriften der Volkskundlichen Kommission für Westfalen, 23 (Münster: Aschendorff, 1976). The songs entered into this manuscript were personally dedicated to the collector, Katharina von Bronchorst und Batenborch, and also written down by herself. Today we would call this manuscript a "poetry album."

> when I composed this little song
> I thought of you very often,
> you are a jewel in my heart,
> if you like me, please let me know,
> send me greetings, it is now your turn.

Sometimes, as in Ottilia No. XXV *Mein freüdt wiewol sie verloschen ist*, here no. 5, a voice in the third person singular underscores the poet's creative contribution, 'She who composed this little song for us, / is called a tender young maid.' Although the use of the third person pronoun "she" implies a certain distance between the actual composer and the performer, this can be explained by the former's attempt to protect herself from possible attacks for having exposed herself in public and for having taken up the pen to write about her own feelings and her personal situation.

Occasionally the female voice reveals a considerable degree of aggression against the disloyal lover, such as in Hätzlerin No. 104 *Ich went, ich hett mir vszerwelt*, here no. 1. Reflecting upon his betrayal and the breaking of his vows to love her forever, she formulates a bitter statement aiming for revenge in the second stanza: 'He broke the promise he gave to me, / this causes me much pain and joy! / I hope I will be revenged / so that I can hurt him badly.' Many times, the poet formulates verses filled with bitterness, disappointment, and frustration as her lover led her astray, such as in Zürich No. 50 *Ich hab mir außerkohren*, here no. 1: 'Who is the person who sang this song to us / who has sung this song anew / this was done by a good virgin / late one evening / she has often sung this song / with a fresh and free mind / she has learned to understand / what the loss of love means.'

Undoubtedly, the composers of these popular songs played with the many different options available to them, and assumed the stance of the sad, betrayed woman who laments the loss of her love, or the role of the bitter, hateful woman who can only think of revenge. At other times they reflect upon their ardent desire to get together again with their lovers, or express their deep sadness resulting from the sorrowful experience of having been separated from their lovers. The last stanza of Zürich No. 53: *DAs ir mich thut verschmähen*, here no. 2, indicates the extent to which we are caught between radical criticism, fully doubting the authenticity of these voices, and positivistic thinking, plainly assuming that because of the female pronoun the song indeed was composed by a woman: 'Herewith I want to come to an end / Oh young man, shining with virtues / do not be cross with me / keep this little song in mind / I have composed it in a hurry / because he has rejected me / I wish you all a good night.'

Ultimately, the question will be whether all these allusions, indica-
tions, and insinuations build enough critical mass to assign this song
indeed to a female poet. Of course, in the light of postmodern thinking,
we might argue, along with Michel Foucault and other deconstruction-
ists, that the quest for the author itself might be entirely outdated and
meaningless, hence also the quest for the female voice.[50] Such a position,
however, would radically undermine all previous efforts to recover the
history of women's literature and to establish a balance between the
genders in terms of creativity, public power and reputation, and self-
presentation. The danger of a return to essentialism then emerges as
imminent. If we knew of a rich tradition of secular women writers in
medieval and early-modern German literature, we might indeed not feel
a need to pursue the question so aggressively of whether the anonymous
songs translated here might be attributable to female poets. This is,
however, as I have outlined in the introduction, not the case, though the
texts by the many mystical writers indicate that female literacy also
existed throughout the Middle Ages.[51] Since many of these religiously
inspired women powerfully demonstrated that they had a superior com-
mand of literary creativity, it seems highly unlikely that other women,
even if they were not members of convents, were entirely unskilled in
this area. Many late-medieval bourgeois and aristocratic girls received a
solid education, and a large portion of secular literature was written for
female audiences.[52] In other words, the search for women writers/poets

---

[50]   Michel Foucault, "What is an Author?," *Contemporary Literary Criticism. Literary and
Cultural Studies*, 2nd ed., Robert Con Davis and Ronald Schleifer, Longman English and
Humanities Series (New York and London: Longman, 1989), 262–75; for a practical appli-
cation of this theoretical construct, see Burt Kimmelman, *The Poetics of Authorship in the
Later Middle Ages. The Emergence of the Modern Literary Persona*, Studies in the
Humanities: Literature—Politics—Society, 21 (New York et al.: Peter Lang, 1996),
94–107, et passim.

[51]   See, for example, *New Trends in Feminine Spirituality. The Holy Women of Liège and their
Impact*, ed. Juliette Dor, Lesley Johnson, and Jocelyn Wogan-Browne, Medieval Women:
Texts and Contexts, 2 (Turnhout: Brepols, 1999); see also the interpretive essay by Ulrike
Wiethaus in: *Agnes Blannbekin, Viennese Beguine: Life and Revelations*, trans. from the
Latin with Introduction, Notes and Interpretive Essay, Library of Medieval Women
(Cambridge: D. S. Brewer, 2002), 163–76.

[52]   Cornelia Niekus Moore, *The Maiden's Mirror: Reading Material for German Girls in
the Sixteenth and Seventeenth Centuries*, Wolfenbütteler Forschungen, 36 (Wiesbaden:
Harrassowitz, 1987); Barbara Becker-Cantarino, *Der lange Weg zur Mündigkeit (1500–
1800)* (Stuttgart: Metzler, 1987), 149–200; Andrea Zupancic, "Kunst und Stadt um 1400,"
*Der Berswordt-Meister und die Dortmunder Malerei um 1400. Stadtkultur im
Spätmittelalter*, ed. Andrea Zupancic and Thomas Schilp (Bielefeld: Verlag für
Regionalgeschichte, 2002), 287–96, here 292; Prudence Allen, RSM, *The Concept of
Woman*, Vol. II: *The Early Humanist Reformation, 1250–1500* (Grand Rapids, MI: William
B. Eerdmans Publishing, 2002), 666–712, offers valuable examples of humanist writing
concerning women's education.

represents a highly important task, and the evidence we have assembled so far indicates that many women actively contributed to the creation of popular song poetry during the fifteenth and sixteenth centuries.

Most important, these women's songs provide significant perspectives as they shed new light on the ancient topic of the erotic relationship between the genders, and they force us to consider women's position more objectively, if possible, at least in stronger contrast to the man's perception as reflected in the dominant canon. In other words, these poems provide a complementary perspective and force us to perceive the topic of love as a crucial medium of discursive exploration of the gender relationship as it occurred in German-speaking lands during the late Middle Ages.[53]

As we learn in *Die maid preist ihren getreuen* (Munich, Staatsbibliothek, Cgm 439), here no. 3, the erotic discourse serves as a platform to outline a complete set of marital ideals:

> It is advisable to be friends with a constant person
> because much joy should grow in us.
> One needs to fight failing constancy.
> Everybody should reflect upon this
> and should consider it and strive
> to develop constancy
> and marry a constant woman.   (118–24)

The poem also indicates the extent to which the female lover has assumed agency and now pursues her own ideals and attempts to satisfy her personal needs in matters of love: 'Most joyfully I have become the girlfriend / of a man whom I have chosen / among all people' (1–3), although she also admits, underscoring the intensity of her passion: 'He is my death, he is my life, / I have handed myself over to him' (15–16). It remains a love poem, however, intense in its treatment of the emotions connecting her with her lover: 'If I could hear his words directly / my heart would be rich with joy, / this I hope every day / and wish him all the best' (92–95). At the same time the female poet also reveals an

---

[53] In *Gender and Text in the Later Middle Ages*, ed. Jane Chance (Gainesville et al.: University Press of Florida, 1996), the contributors offer perspectives on French, Latin, Flemish, Spanish, and English poetry and prose composed by women, whereas the history of German literature seems to be of no relevance in this context. For an example of how to constructively approach this issue, see Albrecht Classen, "Footnotes to the German Canon: Maria von Wolkenstein and Argula von Grumbach," *The Politics of Gender in Early Modern Europe*, ed. Jean R. Brink, Allison P. Coudert and Maryanne C. Horowitz, Sixteenth Century Essays & Studies, XII (Kirksville, MO: Sixteenth Century Journal Publishers, 1989), 131–48; see also my study "Gender Conflicts, Miscommunication, and Communicative Communities in the Late Middle Ages: The Evidence of Fifteenth-Century German Verse Narratives," *Speaking in the Medieval World*, ed. Jean Godsall-Myers, Cultures, Beliefs, and Traditions, 16 (Leiden and Boston: Brill, 2003), 65–92.

underlying fear of losing him again and pleads with him to be loyal and constant in his love for her: 'May God bestow upon him a constant mind / in proper love and constancy' (96–97).

Unfortunately, in the final analysis we cannot conclusively prove beyond all doubt that the poems translated here indeed represent the work composed by late-medieval and early-modern women poets. Nevertheless, all indicators considered suggest that we have unearthed a hitherto unknown tradition of German women's secular love poetry. Very similar to the Old Provencal *troubairitz* poetry (twelfth century), and certainly comparable to contemporary sixteenth-century European women's literature, the love songs translated in our anthology provide the strongest evidence available until now in support of the thesis of female creativity. Even if the opposite might be the case, that is, even if male poets had been responsible for these poetic compositions, they provided women a voice to explore their own issues, concerns, and ideals. But by the same token, why should many noble and urban ladies not have turned to writing when there was such a great interest in women's love songs? Moreover, considering the literary activities of the Duchess Eleonore of Austria, the Countess Elisabeth of Saarbrücken-Nassau, and Helene Kottannerin, all three fully accomplished fifteenth-century women writers,[54] nothing contradicts the claim that these anonymous women songs were indeed composed by women poets.

I would like to conclude this portion of my essay with a brief reference to an intriguing parallel case which is, however, in medieval Persian literature. Rabe'eh Qozdari (latter part of the tenth century), who was born near Balkh in Afghanistan, reflected upon her unhappy love experience and used the poetic genre to launch a bitter invective against her former suitor:

> My hope's that God will make you fall in love
> With someone cold and callous just like you
> And that you'll realize my true value when
> You're twisting in the torments I've been through.[55]

---

[54] Ursula Liebertz-Grün, "Höfische Autorinnen. Von der karolingischen Kulturreform bis zum Humanismus," *Deutsche Literatur von Frauen*, Vol. 1: *Vom Mittelalter bis zum Ende des 18. Jahrhunderts*, ed. Gisela Brinker-Gabler (Munich: Beck, 1988), 48–63; Albrecht Classen, "Women in 15th-Century Literature: Protagonists (Melusine), Poets (Elisabeth von Nassau-Saarbrücken), and Patrons (Mechthild von Österreich)," *"Der Buchstab tödt – der Geist macht lebendig"*. *Festschrift zum 60. Geburtstag von Hans-Gert Roloff*, ed. James Hardin and Jörg Jungmayr, vol. I (Bern, Berlin, Frankfurt a.M. et al.: Lang, 1992), 431–58.

[55] Quoted from Dick Davis, ed., *Borrowed Ware: Medieval Persian Epigrams*, Poetica, 6 (London: Anvil Press Poetry, 1996), 53; I would like to thank my colleague Kamran Talattof, University of Arizona, for alerting me to this marvelous example of medieval Persian women's poetry.

Would we be justified in identifying Qozdari's complaint as a universal theme characteristic of women's problems at all times? It seems striking that twelfth-century Old Occitan *troubairitz* poems, thirteenth-century women *trouvères*, fifteenth- and sixteenth-century German women's poetry, and this medieval Persian song share the same concern—women being abandoned by their lovers whom they aggressively lambast for their disloyalty and whom they hope will experience the same unhappiness in their next love affair as the singer is going through because of his unfaithfulness.[56]

Religious poetry
In contrast with the secular songs, the religious or church songs translated in the present collection normally represent irrefutable cases of female authorship, as both the name of the female poet and the historical context pertaining to the creation of these songs are well-known. This, however, does not make our task easier, though the problems to be tackled are of a different nature. For instance, it proves to be a highly complex challenge to verify the authorship of some of these poets. Even if we think that we know for sure the name of the composer, many vexing questions remain. I will illustrate this with the case of Mary, Queen of Hungary, below. Next, there is no easy way, if any, to relate an individual song by a female poet with female approaches to the spiritual. In many cases the text simply reflects a deep sense of religiosity, or a thorough familiarity with a particular Biblical account. We face serious difficulties in identifying gender-specific elements in the song's content. Some of these songs appear to have been created under the influence of mystical visions, but the differences between them and traditional mystical documents, such as Mechthild of Magdeburg's *The Flowing Light of the Godhead* (ca. 1250–70), are considerable.[57] Nevertheless, a certain tendency toward a mystical discourse, even if the poets never talk about true visionary experiences, can be detected. Finally, we observe that many of these songs were created as private reflections and were not intended for publication. This, however, does not diminish their literary quality; instead we are invited to investigate the songs' religious, social, rhetorical, ideological, and stylistic purposes.

---

[56]   See also the excellent discussion of the same topic in *Songs of the Women Trouvères*, ed. Eglal Doss-Quinby et al., especially with regard to women's voices in the Mozarabic *kharjas*, 13–14.

[57]   Elizabeth Alvilda Petroff, *Medieval Women's Visionary Literature* (New York and Oxford: Oxford University Press, 1986), provides an excellent discussion and good English translations of a vast array of women's mystical texts.

Mary, Queen of Hungary, is acclaimed for having composed the famous church song "Mag ich Unglück nicht widerstan" ('I cannot fight against misfortune') shortly after her young husband, Louis (Lajos), King of Hungary, had died in the battle of Mohács against the victorious Turks in 1526.[58] As early as 1878, A. F. W. Fischer offered an overview of the major arguments in favor of or against Mary's authorship.[59] The song already appeared in print in 1526 shortly after the tragedy of the battle of Mohács, and the broadsheet clearly attributed this song to the widowed Queen. The second printing, by Georg Wachter in Nuremberg, repeated this information and added a second song allegedly composed by Mary, 'Oh God, what am I to sing, my joy is far removed' (*Ach Gott was soll ich singen, Mein freud die ist mir ferr*). The first comprehensive Lutheran church songbook, commissioned by Luther himself and compiled by Joseph Klug in 1529, *Geistliche lieder auffs new gebessert zu Wittemberg*, also contained Mary's first song. Luther carefully assigned the authors' names to most of the songs, especially making sure he received credit for his own works to avoid the problem of being publicly identified with texts other than his own, but Mary's song is not identified by name.[60] Subsequent songbooks, such as the Erfurt Songbook (1531, *Geistliche lieder auffs new gebessert ec.*), followed this tradition, but soon omitted to mention her name again. Mary is first fully identified as the poet of this song in the Low German Magdeburg Songbook from 1534, and most subsequent compilers repeated this attribution.[61] Johann Caspar Wetzel, the

---

[58] Pál Engel, *The Realm of St Stephen. A History of Medieval Hungary, 895–1526*, trans. Tamás Pálosfalvi, English edition ed. Andrew Ayton (London and New York: I. B. Tauris Publishers, 2001), 367–71; for further readings, see 427–29.

[59] A. F. W. Fischer, *Kirchenlieder-Lexikon. Hymnologisch-literarische Nachweisungen über ca. 4500 der wichtigsten und verbreitetsten Kirchenlieder aller Zeiten in alphabetischer Folge nebst einer Übersicht der Liederdichter*, 2 vols. (1878; Hildesheim: Georg Olms, 1967), 45–46.

[60] Markus Jenny, "Luthers Gesangbuch," *Leben und Werk Martin Luthers von 1526–1546. Festgabe zu seinem 500. Geburtstag*, ed. Helmar Junghans (Göttingen: Vandenhoeck & Ruprecht, 1983), 303–21. Why Jenny identifies Albrecht von Preußen as the poem's creator remains completely mysterious. For a facsimile edition, see *Das Klug'sche Gesangbuch 1533*, nach dem einzigen erhaltenen Exemplar der Lutherhalle zu Wittenberg ergänzt und heausgegeben von Konrad Ameln, Documenta Musicologica, Erste Reihe: Druckschriften-Faksimiles, XXV (Kassel, Basel, and London: Bärenreiter, 1983), with the relevant statement about name identification on p. A vi r(ecto); Christian Möller, "Das 16. Jahrhundert," *Kirchenlied und Gesangbuch. Quellen zu ihrer Geschichte. Ein hymnologisches Arbeitsbuch*, ed. Christian Möller, Mainzer hymnologische Studien, 1 (Tübingen and Basel: Francke, 2000), 69–127, here 77, is not quite correct in his claim that all songs, at least those by poets other than Luther, are identified by name.

[61] An exception was *Psalmen vnd Geistliche lieder / welche von fromen Christen gemacht vnd zu samen gelesen sind* (Leipzig: Valentin Babst, 1545); for a facsimile, see *Das Babstsche Gesangbuch von 1545*, facsimile with Preface, ed. Konrad Ameln, Documenta Musicologica,

author of a multi-volume collection of hymns (*Hymnopoeographia*, 1719–28), reported that an old manuscript, dating from Luther's times, contained Mary's song and explicitly credited her with being the composer. In 1759, Johann Bartholomäus Riederer, however, raised doubts and pointed out that the mentioning of Mary's name could have various meanings, either that she had composed it herself, or that she had enjoyed singing it, or that it had been dedicated to her (by a male poet). Fischer questions the validity of all three arguments, as her authorship could neither be verified nor falsified at all. In 1620, Abraham Scultetus assumed that Martin Luther, famous for his own church songs, had composed 'I cannot fight against misfortune' and dedicated it to Mary out of respect for her grief over the loss of her husband. Other authors followed his lead, as it seemed more likely that the powerful leader of the Protestant Reformation was responsible for this remarkable church song, especially as he himself had composed the earliest and most influential Protestant hymns.[62] But since Luther's signature was never added to this song, and as this was the case in all of his other church songs, this claim does not hold water. At the same time no firm and fully supportable evidence against Mary was ever brought to light, despite many authors' attempts to discredit the Hungarian Queen altogether as a poet. Attempts to strengthen the opposite arguments were not much more successful, as comparisons of the song's musical meter with those of other songs by her two relatives, Casimir of Brandenburg and Margrave George, both contained, along with her song, for example, in the *Klugsche Gesangbuch* from 1533, did not yield many results.

Interestingly, a number of secular songs have come down to us that use the same first line as the song by Queen Mary, which confirms the popularity of this religious song. Philip Nicolai composed a religious song in 1596 which begins with the same words in the first verse, "Mag ich Unglück nicht widerstahn," but otherwise no further similarities can be observed.[63] Significantly, Nicolai's name appears at the end of the poem, whereas Mary's name is normally mentioned at the top of the text or hidden within the poem through the use of an acrostic.[64] Recent research has not gained any new insights either way, but we have learned

---

Erste Reihe: Druckschriften-Faksimiles, XXXVIII (Kassel, Basel, London, and New York: Bärenreiter, 1988), 2nd part, no. xvii; here the title only says: "Ein ander geistlich lied" ('Another religious song'), which represents a very common practice in sixteenth-century church songbooks.

[62]   Christian Möller, "Das 16. Jahrhundert," 70–85.

[63]   This song is contained in Nicolai's essay *Nohtwendiger vnd gantz vollkommener Bericht: Von der gantzen Caluinischen Religion* (Frankfurt a.M., 1596), 357.

[64]   A. F. W. Fischer, *Kirchenlieder-Lexikon*, II, 47.

better to understand Mary's considerable education, her astounding political influence on Hungary, and later on the Netherlands which she governed on behalf of her brother, Emperor Charles V from 1531 until 1555 when she retired to Spain. She enjoyed some contact with Martin Luther whose texts she studied closely and who composed four psalms for her soon after the battle of Mohács and her husband's death. In 1533, when she was already serving as governor of the Netherlands, she invited Erasmus of Rotterdam to return to his home country, but he had already died in 1536 while still living in Basel. He dedicated his treatise *Vidua christiana* (1529; 'The Christian Widow') to her. Mary was also famous for her great interest in music and the major intellectual questions of her time.[65]

Ursula Tamussino recently published a biography of Queen Mary and also considered the question of whether she had composed this church song herself.[66] Although Tamussino acknowledges Mary's outstanding level of education, her great interest in the arts, and her passion for music, she casts serious doubt on the possibility that the widow might have penned this song herself. Tamussino copies several versions of this song, and also mentions that some scholars attributed it to Martin Luther, but she refrains from any final decision: "Luther's authorship is possible, but not proven, just as much or as little as Mary's authorship."[67] The intriguing issue here is that Mary's song certainly implies a leaning toward Protestantism, whereas the House of Hapsburg was adamantly opposed to the Reformation. Mary's brother, Ferdinand, at that time ruler over the Hapsburgian lands, served as a proxy for his brother Emperor Charles V.[68] He severely reprimanded his sister when he had received a copy of Luther's dedication to Mary in the prologue to his four psalms which were written for her. Mary cleverly responded and defended herself well against the charge of having become a secret convert to Protestantism, but she never stated her clear opposition and did not condemn Luther as a "notorious heretic," as Charles V had labeled him.[69]

Here I assume that Mary indeed composed this song, as I find the evidence of the acrostic with her name convincing enough, especially

[65] Gernot Heiß, "Maria, Erzherzogin von Österreich," *Neue deutsche Biographie*, vol. 17 (Berlin: Duncker & Humblot, 1990), 207–09; for an excellent website, though in Dutch, see Jeroen Savelkouls' http://www.kun.nl/ahc/vg/html/vg000196.html

[66] Ursula Tamussino, *Maria von Ungarn. Ein Leben im Dienst der Casa de Austria* (Graz, Vienna, and Cologne: Verlag Styria, 1998).

[67] Tamussino, 133.

[68] http://www.bautz.de/bbkl/f/ferdinand_i_r_k.shtml

[69] Tamussino, 135–37.

considering the circumstances and Mary's interest in literature and the arts: "MA" introduces the first line of the first stanza, "RI" the first line of the second stanza, and the capital "A" stands at the beginning of the first line of the third stanza. The song demonstrates her personal suffering resulting from her husband's death. She expresses that she cannot fight back misery imposed upon her, but she trusts that God would protect her in the long run. In fact, He will, as she states, soon strangle those who prevent her from reading His own words, the Bible. Although she realizes her personal weakness (referring to her status as a woman), she is confident that those who are mighty in this world will eventually fall down, as no temporary power would last forever. Consequently, she is searching for spiritual truth and is willing to risk all her material property and even her own life to aspire to this goal. The poet expresses her unconditional trust in Christ as her savior and helper in all her suffering, as He would consider her pain as if it were His own.

In the case of Agnes, Duchess of Saxony, no serious doubt about her authorship comes into play. In the subtitle of the song "ACh Gott, an einem morgen," printed in 1553 in Dresden, she is explicitly identified as the poet. The song itself reveals her name through an acrostic which also mentions her position as Duchess and Elector (the seven German Electors elected the German King). The poem is very clear about her personal suffering resulting from her husband's death. She laments, while looking at his corpse on the bier, his early death. She sings a song in praise of his accomplishments and military efforts to bring peace to Germany and to chase away marauding and pillaging troops. His death means, as she emphasizes, deep pain for herself and her child, and she would have been glad to give up all her power and lands to save his life. Agnes composed a moving poem, giving vent to her grief and her desperation. Nevertheless, at the end she formulates her trust in God and indicates how much her religious devotion will help her to survive her deep pain.

The fairly large collection of religious and didactic songs by Elisabeth, Duchess of Brunswick-Lüneburg proves to be similarly moving.[70] In "Allein gott in der hohe sei ehr" ('God alone in the highest be given honor'), here no. 8, for instance, the poet reveals her maternal instincts and her profound love for her daughter Catharina. Because of her daughter,

[70] For a very brief discussion, see Barbara Becker-Cantarino, "Renaissance oder Reformation? Epochenschwellen für schreibende Frauen und die Mittlere Deutsche Literatur," *Das Berliner Modell der Mittleren Deutschen Literatur. Beiträge zur Tagung Kloster Zinna 29.9.–01.10. 1997*, ed. and introduced by Christiane Caemmerer, Walter Delabar, et al., Chloe, 33 (Amsterdam and Atlanta: Editions Rodopi, 2000), 69–87, here 84.

Elisabeth has gained enough strength to support herself in a world hostile to her. She uses the song both as a general appeal to Christ to protect Catharina who has lost her father, and to secure for her a trustworthy and supportive husband. The mother also emphasizes that her daughter loves no one more ardently than her mother and God Himself. In the fifth stanza, Elisabeth describes her daughter's upbringing and maturation, and entrusts her care to Christ. Finally, she turns to Catharina directly and offers her concrete advice on how to fare in this world, that is, to love her mother and to honor God. As the song's title and the concluding verse indicate, Elisabeth composed this song for a special occasion, the First Advent of 1554. It is a passionate poem in many respects, not least because of its highly personal approach and direct address to the daughter. Elisabeth succeeds in combining many different concerns, such as her relationship with her daughter, love for God, the need for divine protection especially in the case of Catharina who has lost her father, and didactic teachings for her daughter. Despite its highly intimate and individualized approach, 'God alone in the highest be given honor' proves to be a remarkable expression of women's issues during the late Middle Ages and of female religiosity in particular.

Remarkably, many, if not all of these women's religious songs serve to establish a direct connection between the poet and the Godhead. As Magdalena Bekin states in the first stanza of her song 'Can there never be any alternative,'

> Oh God, have mercy on me!
> Am I the only one who experiences misfortune today?
> Lord, take me into your protection
> and turn away from me
> through Your divine grace
> the cross that I have to bear.
> Lord, you know well what it takes.

She and many other women poets experienced, it seems, existential threats and resorted to God as their last support. The poetic framework provided them with a significant outlet for their fears and helped them and their audiences to regain confidence and trust. This is powerfully expressed by Marie Cleopha, Countess of Sulz, in her poem 'Oh God in the Highest' (no. 1):

> Oh God in the Highest,
> trustingly I am calling upon You,
> just as you have told me to do,
> please do not abandon me.

She also imagines herself as suffering the same way as Christ did, being despised, rejected, and persecuted here in this world. While appealing

for His support, she also assumes the role of a successor to Christ who
has to undergo similar sacrifices:

> Wherever I turn
> I am despised:
> at every place here on Earth
> nothing else counts but violence and money   (stanza 5)

The poet uses her song as a medium to reach out to Christ and to call
for his help in her own misery: 'I cry out to God / both day and night'
(no. 2, 3). Marie Cleopha formulates a quasi mystical vision, though she
experiences so much pain because she is not graced with an actual rev-
elation. The song, however, serves to establish a link with the Godhead
and to secure his direct support: 'He keeps me alive / through His
might' (no. 2, 3), particularly because the poet perceives herself sur-
rounded by dangers and threats, especially originating from Satan who
is about to attack her:

> Rescue me, God,
> from the devil's might
> when his bitter death
> will strike me.   (no. 2, 8)

In their religious quest these women poets developed powerful poetic
images and convincingly formulated their desires, fears, and apprehen-
sions resulting from difficult, dangerous, painful, and sometimes cata-
strophic situations. It would be very challenging to identify specifically
female themes, language, or concerns, as the overriding impetus proves
to be the request to reach out to the Godhead and to secure His help at
a time of great turmoil with military and economic threats.[71] But with
respect to these religious songs the poets' gender does not seem to be
the decisive factor for the critical examination of the content. What
matters, by contrast, is the simple observation that these women com-
posed so many religious songs and that they were more or less recog-
nized by their male contemporaries for their contribution to the genre
of the hymn. Whereas current scholarship has not yet paid adequate
attention to this phenomenon,[72] we can now affirm that the history of

---

[71] For a history of women's conditions in the late Middle Ages, see Barbara Becker-Cantarino,
Der lange Weg zur Mündigkeit. Frau und Literatur (1500–1800) (Stuttgart: Metzler, 1987),
48–65; *Women in Reformation and Counter-Reformation Europe. Public and Private Worlds*,
ed. Sherrin Marshall (Bloomington and Indianapolis: Indiana University Press, 1989).

[72] Christian Möller, "Das 16. Jahrhundert," 87–88, mentions only Katharina Zell's songbook *Von
Christo Jesu unserem säligmacher* from 1534 and ignores all other women poets; this absolute
dearth applies to all other chapters in this volume, and thus to hymnological research at large;
the only remarkable exception, though not fully scholarly in its approach, seems to be
Elisabeth Schneider-Böklen, *Der Herr hat Großes mir getan. Frauen im Gesangbuch*, 2nd ed.
(1995; Stuttgart: Quell, 1997); Albrecht Classen, *'Mein Seel fang an zu singen'*.

sixteenth-century German literature also witnessed a remarkable emergence of female poets.

The Protestant Reformation proved to be liberating for some of them; for others the institutionalization of the Protestant Church also meant a new barrier for them, such as reflected by Anna Ovena Hoyers (1584–1655). She was severely persecuted by the authorities for her radical poetic statements in which she harshly criticized local ministers and attacked the orthodox hierarchy for its lack of religious enlightenment.[73] Nuns, some of them already converted to Protestantism, also became active as composers of religious poetry and hymns, such as Anna of Quernheim (before 1520–90),[74] but even during the following centuries only a few names were recorded or have possibly not yet been discovered by modern scholarship.[75] The wealth of archival material, however, both in public and private libraries, in convents and other institutions, promises many new discoveries of women's poetry and hymns. The considerable number of texts included in our translation indicates that the present gender imbalance in the history of late-medieval and early-modern German literature might be due more to patriarchal attitudes among modern-day scholarship and its traditional ignorance of non-canonical texts than to an actual absence of women poets.

Outlook

Can we assume that the chorus of female voices presented here implies that many more women poets from the Middle Ages could be discovered? Possibly, but we have no certainty, especially as the archives do not easily yield new documents and names. After about two hundred years of intensive philological research, it seems clear that medieval German women were not much involved in the writing of courtly romances or courtly love poetry during the twelfth and thirteenth centuries. However,

---

[73] I have not included her texts here because they fall into different genres; see Albrecht Classen, *Frauen in der deutschen Literaturgeschichte. Die ersten 800 Jahre. Ein Lesebuch*, Women in German Literature, 4 (New York: Peter Lang, 2000), 250–73; ibid., "Die 'Querelle des femmes' im 16. Jahrhundert im Kontext des theologischen Gelehrtenstreits: Die literarischen Beiträge von Argula von Grumbach und Anna Ovena Hoyers," *Wirkendes Wort* 50, 2 (2000): 189–213; for an introduction to Hoyers in English, see Barbara Becker-Cantarino, "Anna Ovena Hoyers," *German Baroque Writers, 1580–1660*, ed. James Hardin, Dictionary of Literary Biographies, 164 (Detroit, Washington, DC, and London: Gale Research, 1996), 181–84.

[74] Gertrud Angermann, *Anna von Quernheim (vor 1520–1590). Die erste bekannte Liederdichterin Westfalens und 25 ihrer geistlichen Gesänge in niederdeutscher Sprache* (Bielefeld: Aisthesis, 1996).

[75] See the short list in my *'Mein Seelfang an zu singen'*, 13–14, which I created on the basis of Albert Fischer's *Das deutsche evangelische Kirchenlied des 17. Jahrhunderts*, completed and edited by W. Tümpel, 6 vols, rpt. (1904–16; Hildesheim: Georg Olms, 1964).

new questions, new methodological approaches, and new investigative tools might help us, as the collection of women's songs in our translation indicates, to uncover new traditions. Perhaps German women relied more on oral tradition during the high Middle Ages, which would make it extremely difficult to retrieve their works today. Perhaps they used pseudonyms, or perhaps they expressed themselves in literary forms that conform to specific genres that do not allow the poet to leave any gender markers or autobiographical elements, which prevents us today from easily identifying their works as texts composed by women. The wealth of literary documents presented here at least gives us sufficient reason to anticipate further discoveries. Neither the thirteenth nor the fourteenth century has been studied thoroughly enough, and perhaps the time has come to re-examine the large poetry collections from those periods in our quest for unknown women writers. At least, the present results strongly suggest that fifteenth- and sixteenth-century women were highly active in composing secular and religious songs. In conclusion, there remain many opportunities to search beyond the currently available sources in print format and to enrich our understanding of German women's literary history throughout the Middle Ages and the age of the Reformation.

Annotated Bibliography

Since this volume presents authentic late-medieval and early-modern German women's songs for the first time in English translation, it will be difficult for those readers who do not read German to find relevant studies published in English. Moreover, the texts selected for translation are either taken from archival sources or copied from mostly nineteenth-century editions published by scholars who still had access to private libraries and other collections which now are either lost or inaccessible. Fortunately, international research on premodern women writers has made tremendous progress, which is reflected in the large number of significant critical studies on French, Italian, English, and Latin writers. This bibliography highlights some of the most important research that contributes to our understanding of German women's poetry from an interdisciplinary and historical perspective which deliberately does not draw rigid demarcation lines between the Middle Ages and the early-modern period.

Primary texts

Angermann, Gertrud. *Anna von Quernheim (vor 1520–1590). Die erste bekannte Liederdichterin Westfalens und 25 ihrer geistlichen Gesänge in niederdeutscher Sprache* **(Bielefeld: Aisthesis Verlag, 1996).**
  This is an edition of twenty-five church songs composed by Anna von Quernheim, the first known Westphalian woman writer. Angermann introduces the edition with a biographical sketch, a study of Anna's theology, an analysis of her poetry and its sources, and a discussion of her life as Abbess. The poems are edited on the basis of the only extant print copy in the Herzog August Library, Wolfenbüttel, in the original early-modern Low German and translated into modern German on the facing pages.

Anna von Köln. *Liederbuch der Anna von Köln (um 1500),* **ed. Walter Salmen and Johannes Koepp, Denkmäler rheinischer Musik, 4 (Düsseldorf: L. Schwann, 1954).**
  Anna, a nun in a Cologne convent, was the first owner of this songbook. Eighty-two songs, apparently copied down by various hands, make up this songbook which is influenced by mystical thoughts. Only three (male) composers are known to us: Thomas à Kempis, Johann Brugmann, and

Martin Luther. The female scribes copied a wide range of religious songs from a variety of sources, but thirty-five of them are unique to this collection. Although it seems unlikely that the nuns created their own songs, this *Liederbuch* reflects women's strong interest in religious song-poetry and supports the claim that our text selection was indeed composed by female poets. Salmen and Koepp edited and commented on the songs. In German.

Bergliederbüchlein. Historisch-kritische Ausgabe, ed. Elizabeth Mincoff-Marriage, together with Gerhard Heilfurth, Bibliothek des literarischen Vereins in Stuttgart, CCLXXXV (Leipzig: Hiersemann, 1936).

When the mining industry began to flourish north of the Alps during the sixteenth century, many miners also composed songs about their own world. Nevertheless, this miner's songbook is not exclusively dedicated to mining and contains a wide range of popular songs, some of which seem to have been composed by women as well. Historical-critical edition of this songbook. In German.

Birlinger, A. "Strassburgisches Liederbuch," *Alemannia* 1 (1875): 1–59.

Ottilia Fenchlerin lived in sixteenth-century Strassburg and commissioned the scribe Caspar Schröpfer to create a songbook for her (completed on May 22, 1592). Although most songs are anonymous, a large percentage fall into the category of women's songs. There are two major strategies pursued by the poets: either the narrative voice identifies herself as female, without revealing her name, or the song's content specifically addresses female concerns and interests. Birlinger provides some general introductory remarks and edits the manuscript. This is not a historical-critical edition; Birlinger only points out in which other songbooks individual songs had been copied. In German.

Agnes Blannbekin, Viennese Beguine: Life and Revelations, trans. from the Latin with Introduction, Notes and Interpretive Essay by Ulrike Wiethaus, Library of Medieval Women (Cambridge: D. S. Brewer, 2002).

Apart from Wilbirg of St. Florian, Agnes (d. 1315) was the only mystical visionary in medieval Austria. Her revelations are here translated by Wiethaus into English for the first time, who also offers a thorough discussion of the literary-historical and theological context. The significance of this mystical account rests in the fact that it demonstrates, as in the case of many other mystical women writers such as Hildegard of Bingen and Mechthild of Magdeburg, that medieval women actively participated in the creation of literature, even if they were limited to religious texts. On the basis of this mystical literature we gain solid support for the claim that many late-medieval women in Germany also authored secular love songs and church songs.

Classen, Albrecht. *Deutsche Frauenlieder des 15. und 16. Jahrhunderts,* **Amsterdamer Publikationen zur Sprache und Literatur, 136 (Amsterdam and Atlanta: Editions Rodopi, 1999).**
This is an edition of secular love songs apparently composed by fifteenth- and sixteenth-century German women writers. These songs can be found in many different songbooks, but they have come down to us anonymously. The determining factor for inclusion in this edition was whether a truly female voice ("I, virgin . . . ") confirms at the end of a song that she composed it, or whether the content strongly suggests female authorship. This edition also provides some text examples and information about significant religious songbooks copied by late-medieval nuns. The selection of secular women's love poetry translated in the present volume is taken from this edition. A lengthy introduction offers in-depth information about the genre of late-medieval songbooks and the role of women in the history of medieval German literature. In German.

——. *'Mein Seel fang an zu singen'. Religiöse Frauenlieder des 15.–16. Jahrhunderts,* **Studies in Spirituality Supplement (Leuven: Peeters, 2002).**
Religiously inspired women mostly identified themselves as the authors of their own songs either by signing with their name or by employing an acrostic. These are re-edited in this anthology, along with several church songbooks copied by nuns in the convents of Wienhausen (near Celle, Northern Germany), Ebstorf (near Uelzen, Northern Germany), and Niesing (Münster, Northwest Germany), the latter copied by Catharina Tirs. Most poets were high-ranking Protestant noble ladies, but some were school teachers (Magdalena Heymairin) or wives of ministers and professors (Elisabeth Crucigerin). The introduction focuses on the development of the churchsong in early-modern Germany, and each chapter offers detailed biographical sketches and historical background, especially with respect to the women's convents where some of the most important songbooks were copied down, such as in Wienhausen. In German.

Die Darnfelder Liederhandschrift 1546–1565, **based on initial work by Arthur Hübner und Ada-Elise Beckmann, ed. Rolf Wilhelm Brednich, Schriften der Volkskundlichen Kommission für Westfalen, 23 (Münster: Aschendorff, 1976).**
Kathryna of Bronchorst and Batenborch created the first German poetry album during the second half of the sixteenth century. She herself and many relatives, friends, her later husband, and guests jotted down popular songs they knew by heart. Some of these belong to the category of women's songs. Brednich discusses the manuscript, its historical context, the language of the poems, and identifies other songbooks which also include parallel copies of a specific song. This is a historical-critical edition. In German.

Jörg Dürnhofers Liederbuch (um 1515). Faksimile des Liedruck-Sammelbandes Inc. **1446a der Universitätsbibliothek Erlangen, with epilogue and commentary by Frieder Schanze, Fortuna Vitrea, 11 (Tübingen: Niemeyer, 1993).**

The Eichstätt citizen Jörg Dürnhofer created one of the earliest German songbooks. He was a clothmaker and assumed various posts in the city government between 1469, when he received his citizenship, and his death in 1503. Dürnhofer collected individual songs printed as single broadsheets and bound them together. His son Lienhard moved to Nuremberg and probably took the songbook with him. It is today housed in the University Library of Erlangen and contains a wide selection of religious and secular songs. The editor published this songbook as a facsimile and added detailed comments on each song. In German.

(Elisabeth). Goltz, Freiherr von der Goltz-Greifswald, "Lieder der Herzogin Elisabeth von Braunschweig-Lüneburg, Gräfin von Henneberg zu Hannover von 1553 bis 1555 gedichtet," *Zeitschrift der Gesellschaft für niedersächsische Kirchengeschichte* **19 (1914): 147–208.**

This article offers, along with biographical and historical information, an edition of fifteen songs by the Duchess Elisabeth of Braunschweig-Lüneburg (1510–1558). She converted to Protestantism after her husband's death in 1540 and introduced the new religion in her territory. When her son Erich II assumed the government in 1546, he tried to reintroduce Catholicism, causing much internal strife. His mother experienced many conflicts with financial creditors and was even imprisoned once because she could not pay back a debt to the city of Hanover for which she had been the guarantor. Elisabeth wrote mostly religious poems, but she also addressed her daughter directly in order to give her ethical, moral, and religious advice. In German.

Forster, Georg. *Frische Teutsche Liedlein (1539–1556),* **Five vols., ed. Kurt Gudewill, Hinrich Siuts (co-ed. vol. 2) , Horst Brunner (co-ed. vols. 3–5). Das Erbe deutscher Musik. Erste Reihe: Reichsdenkmale, 20, 60–63 (Wolfenbüttel: Möseler Verlag, 1964–97).**
M. Elizabeth Marriage. *Georg Forsters Frische teutsche Liedlein. Abdruck nach den ersten Ausgaben 1539, 1540, 1549, 1556 und den Abweichungen der späteren Drucke,* **Neudrucke deutscher Literaturwerke des XVI. und XVII. Jahrhunderts, 203–206 (Halle: Niemeyer, 1903).**

Both editions of Forster's songbooks need to be consulted, as they emphasize different aspects. Gudewill and his co-editors provide the score sheets, accompanied by the texts, whereas Marriage offers only the texts without the scores. Georg Forster, a medical doctor and humanist in Nuremberg, collected popular songs, such as love songs, didactic songs, political and historical ballads, and also some religious songs, between 1539 and 1556 and published them in five volumes. The early volumes enjoyed tremendous popularity and were reprinted many times, whereas the later ones experienced less success, indicating a considerable change in public taste. Both publications are in German.

Goedeke, Karl and Julius Tittmann. *Liederbuch aus dem sechzehnten Jahrhundert.* **Deutsche Dichter des sechzehnten Jahrhunderts, 1 (Leipzig: Brockhaus, 1867).**
Many sixteenth-century songbooks are no longer available or extremely difficult to find even in German archives. Goedeke's and Tittmann's edition provides a very important selection of songs copied nowhere else, and include several women's songs. In German.

Liederbuch der Clara Hätzlerin, **based on a Manuscript in the Bohemian Museum in Prague, trans. and with an introduction and glossary by Carl Halthaus, Bibliothek der gesammten deutschen National-Literatur, 8 (Quedlinburg and Leipzig: Gottfr. Basse, 1840; rpt. with an epilogue by Hanns Fischer, Berlin: de Gruyter, 1966).**
On behalf of the Augsburg Patrician Jörg Roggenburg, the professional scribe Clara Hätzlerin composed this songbook in 1471. It contains a wide selection of fourteenth- and fifteenth-century poetry, some of which was obviously composed by women. This large volume reflects the general literary taste and interest in popular and also highly sophisticated German poetry among late-medieval urban and aristocratic audiences. Whereas Halthaus published a straightforward edition of the text, Hanns Fischer discussed the songbook in the 1966 reprint in the light of modern research, focusing on the dissemination and significance of these songs. In German.

Das Liederbuch des Johannes Heer von Glarus. Ein Musikheft aus der Zeit des Humanismus (Codex 462 der Stiftsbibliothek St. Gallen, **ed. Arnold Geering and Hans Trümpy, Schweizerische Musikdenkmäler, 5 (Basel: Bärenreiter, 1967).**
This songbook was produced by an early sixteenth-century Swiss humanist. Although he was deeply concerned with humanism and the Reformation as espoused by Ulrich Zwingli, his interest in popular song poetry was quite traditional. He also included several women's songs. The songs are presented with their scores and the accompanying texts. In German.

The Memoirs of Helene Kottanner (439–1440), **trans. from the German with Introduction, Interpretive Essay and Notes by Maya Bijvoet Williamson, Library of Medieval Women (Cambridge and Rochester, NY: D. S. Brewer, 1999).**
The first book of memoirs in the history of German literature was written by the royal chambermaid Helene Kottanner (or Kottannerin). Previously considered to be merely a historical document, recent investigations led to the realization that this text has a tremendous significance

for late-medieval German literature. Bijvoet Williamson offers a meticulous English translation, introduces the author, and discusses the historical context. The volume concludes with an insightful interpretive essay.

Lewis, Gertrud Jaron. *By Women, for Women, about Women. The Sister-Books of Fourteenth-Century Germany*, **Studies and Texts, 125 (Toronto: Pontifical Institute of Mediaeval Studies, 1996).**
Fourteenth-century Southwest German women's convents were important centers of Dominican mysticism. Lewis offers a detailed literary and theological study of the genre of *sister-books*, consisting of many individual visionary accounts, and provides a copy of all relevant texts on microfiche. All passages quoted in the text are rendered into English.

Mechthild of Magdeburg. *The Flowing Light of the Godhead*, **trans. and introduced by Frank Tobin (New York and Mahwah: Paulist Press, 1998).**
For the most magisterial English translation of the Low German mystic Mechthild of Magdeburg, one needs to consult Frank Tobin's work. Mechthild's visionary accounts prove to be outstanding literary creations and confirm once again that medieval German women certainly had opportunities to write and compose poetry if they gained the necessary freedom either as a beguine or as a nun and the authority to write through their mystical visions.

Meier, Max. *Das Liederbuch Ludwig Iselins* **(Basel: Werner-Riehm, 1913).**
Unfortunately never reprinted, Max Meier's doctoral dissertation offers a critical text edition of the songbook by the Swiss humanist Ludwig Iselin. As in the case of Johannes Heer, this collection demonstrates that popular songs appealed to a diverse audience, including the humanists. The edition includes a highly informative introduction to Iselin and his career. Meier describes the manuscript and its date, describes the language used by the collector/scribe, analyzes the dominant metrical forms, discusses the songs' content, and explores their origins. This is not a historical-critical edition. In German.

Merkel, Kerstin, and Heide Wunder, eds. *Deutsche Frauen der Frühen Neuzeit. Dichterinnen, Malerinnen, Mäzeninnen* **(Darmstadt: Primus, 2000).**
The contributors offer solid overviews and detailed studies of seven women writers, three women painters, and five women patrons in the history of early-modern German literature. The focus rests on the seventeenth and eighteenth centuries, when women managed to gain major inroads into male domains, such as architecture, landscape architecture, painting, and art collection—and there were many important women writers. Most of these women here receive, for almost the first time, full scholarly attention, whereas the articles on sixteenth-century women writers reintroduce well-known names.

Mützell, Julius, ed. *Geistliche Lieder der Evangelischen Kirche aus dem sechszehnten* **(sic)** *Jahrhundert, nach den ältesten Drucken*, **3 vols. (Berlin: Th. Chr. Fr. Enslin, 1855).**

Intended to supplement Wackernagel's monumental edition of late-medieval and early-modern religious songs (see below), Julius Mützell's edition contains a large selection of sixteenth-century Protestant church songs. In German.

Petroff, Elizabeth Alvilda, ed., *Medieval Women's Visionary Literature* **(New York and Oxford: Oxford University Press, 1986).**

Petroff's comprehensive anthology of medieval women's mystical, or visionary, literature in English translation covers European women's texts from late antiquity to the fifteenth century. All major women mystics and other female religious authors are represented. In her introduction, Petroff discusses the phenomenon of female mysticism and analyzes specific features of women's visionary literature.

Rieger, Angelika. Trobairitz. *Der Beitrag der Frau in der altokzitanischen höfischen Lyrik.* **Edition des Gesamtkorpus, Beihefte zur Zeitschrift für Romanische Philologie, 233 (Tübingen: Niemeyer, 1991).**

The Old Occitan women troubadours, the *troubairitz*, represent the most important forerunners of late-medieval German women poets. Rieger's historical-critical edition provides the most reliable and comprehensive text base. Primary texts in Old Occitan accompanied by modern German translations; Rieger's introduction, interpretation, and commentary is in German.

Songs of the Women Trouvères, **ed., trans., and introduced by Eglal Doss-Quinby, Joan Tasker Grimbert, Wendy Pfeffer, and Elizabeth Aubrey (New Haven and London: Yale University Press, 2001).**

As recent research has demonstrated, at least eight women poets can be identified among the North French *trouvères*. Their texts are edited and translated side by side by in this volume. The introduction offers important new insights into medieval women's actual role in literature, music, and the arts. Here we also find a thorough examination of all presently available biographical information, some score sheets, and a discussion of the various poetic genres used by these women poets. *Songs of the Women Trouvères* provides the strongest support yet from an interdisciplinary perspective for the authenticity of the women's songs translated in the present volume, although these Old French poems are about 200 to 250 years older.

Wackernagel, Philipp, ed., *Das deutsche Kirchenlied von der ältesten Zeit bis zu Anfang des XVII. Jahrhunderts*, **5 vols. (Leipzig: Teubner, 1864–1877; rpt. Hildesheim: Georg Olms, 1964).**

From the Protestant Reformation the genre of the church songbook experienced a tremendous proliferation. Wackernagel published the most comprehensive collection on the basis of thorough and extensive archival research. Many of the songbooks that he incorporated in his anthology are no longer accessible (in private collections) or have simply been lost. Wackernagel's biographical, philological, and theological information and explanations are invaluable. Text edition, biographical and other background data, occasionally musical scores. In German.

Wiesner-Hanks, Merry. *Convents Confront the Reformation: Catholic & Protestant Nuns in Germany* introduced and ed. by Merry Wiesner-Hanks, trans. Joan Skocir and Merry Wiesner-Hanks, Reformation Texts with Translation (1350–1650), 1 (Milwaukee: Marquette University, 1996).
During the early years of the Protestant Reformation, a number of Catholic and Protestant women in Germany published pamphlets, treatises, poems, and letters addressing the thorny issue of the reform of the Church, some of which are made available in this edition with facing English translation for the first time. The introduction provides a good historical overview.

Wilson, Katharina. *Hrotsvit of Gandersheim: A Florilegium of her Works*, trans. with Introduction, Interpretive Essay and Notes, Library of Medieval Women (Cambridge: D. S. Brewer, 1998).
As the English translation of the most important texts by the tenth-century Abbess Hrotsvit indicates, given the opportunity, early-medieval women were fully capable of creating dramas, epic poems, and religious legends, using Latin as the language of the learned. Wilson includes a very insightful introduction and an interpretive essay.

***The Writings of Medieval Women. An Anthology*, 2nd ed., translations and introductions by Marcelle Thiébaux, The Garland Library of Medieval Literature (New York and London: Garland, 1994).**
This is one of the best and most comprehensive anthologies of medieval women's literature in English translation. Thiébaux offers an excellent selection of texts from late antiquity to the fifteenth century, accompanying each chapter with a concise introduction to the individual author. Typically, however, medieval German women's literature is almost completely overlooked, except for Hrotsvitha of Gandersheim and Hildegard of Bingen (both writing in Latin).

Secondary texts

Bainton, Roland Herbert, *Women of the Reformation in Germany and Italy* (Minneapolis: Augsburg Publishing House, 1971).
Bainton provides extensive discussions of sixteenth-century women writers in Germany and Italy who made significant contributions to the development of the Protestant Reformation. Though published as early as 1971, his observations are not yet outdated. This is an excellent introduction to

the large but still little understood topic of women in the Protestant Reformation.

Becker-Cantarino, Barbara, *Der lange Weg zur Mündlichkeit. Frau und Literatur (1500–1800)* **(Stuttgart: Metzler, 1987).**
This is one of the most seminal studies on the history of German women from 1500 to 1800. Although Becker-Cantarino focuses mostly on the seventeenth and eighteenth centuries, she offers detailed examinations of the historical, social, and cultural conditions of sixteenth-century German women of various social classes. The author was not yet aware of the large corpus of popular women's songs and women's church songs during that period, translated in the present volume, but she critically examines a large number of the most important German Baroque and Enlightenment women writers and views them in their cultural-historical context. In German.

Carpenter, Jennifer and Sally-Beth Mac Lean, eds., *Power of the Weak. Studies on Medieval Women* **(Urbana and Chicago: University of Illinois Press, 1995).**
As the title of the essay collection indicates, the contributors suggest that subjugated and marginalized women during the Middle Ages surprisingly exerted considerable political power and subtle yet forceful influence in their private lives; this phenomenon can be observed in the lives of women in the lower social classes and in the lives of queens and other noble ladies. The contributors focus on Anglo-Norman, French, Spanish, and English women.

Classen, Albrecht. *Deutsche Liederbücher des 15. und 16. Jahrhunderts*, **Volksliedstudien, 1 (Münster and New York: Waxmann, 2001).**
The songbook, as it emerged as a new genre during the fifteenth and sixteenth centuries, reflected an astonishingly traditional orientation, whether a songbook was still handwritten or already printed (in individual broadsheets). This study provides a comprehensive overview of the genre and its historical development, and examines twenty of the major songbooks from that period. Each individual song is briefly introduced and analyzed. An index provides an easy search tool for particular motifs and themes. In German.

——. "Ottilia Fenchlerin's Songbook: A Contribution to the History of Sixteenth-Century German Women's Literature," *Women in German Yearbook* **14 (1999): 19–40.**
Comparing Old Occitan *troubairitz* poetry with late-medieval German women's poetry, this article demonstrates, on the basis of a close textual analysis, that most of the songs contained in Ottilia Fenchlerin's songbook were indeed composed by women.

——, *"Ach Gott, wem soll ichs klagen.* Women's Erotic Poetry in Sixteenth-Century German Songbooks," *Neuphilologische Mitteilungen* XCVIII, 3 (1997): 293–318.

> This article represents the first exploration of sixteenth-century German women's poetry contained in a wide variety of songbooks and analyzes a range of poetic examples where female voices emerge, though the texts remain anonymous.

——, **"Female Exploration of Literacy: Epistolary Challenges to the Literary Canon in the Late Middle Ages,"** *Disputatio* 1: *The Late-Medieval Epistle* (1996): 89–121.

> Research into women's literature often depends on the specific approaches and questions asked regarding women's literacy and their chance to get their works published. As this article indicates, letters were often the most important (or only) avenue for women to express themselves in writing. In fact, many women were members of a circle of correspondents, involving family members and friends. Although these late-medieval letters were not destined for public performance, as often was the case in humanists' correspondence, the analysis of a large corpus of German women's letters implies that they relied heavily on the epistolary genre as their only or at least most successful access to literary creativity.

——, **"Women in 15th-Century Literature: Protagonists (Melusine), Poets (Elisabeth von Nassau-Saarbrücken), and Patrons (Mechthild von Österreich),"** *"Der Buchstab tödt—der Geist macht lebendig". Festschrift zum 60. Geburtstag von Hans-Gert Roloff,* ed. **James Hardin and Jörg Jungmayr, vol. I (Bern, Berlin, Frankfurt a.M. et al.: Lang, 1992), 431–58.**

> This article demonstrates that, contrary to general assumptions about their involvement in the world of late-medieval German literature, women could enjoy considerable importance as protagonists in prose narratives, as writers, and as patrons of the arts and literature.

——, ed., *Women as Protagonists and Poets in the German Middle Ages. An Anthology of Feminist Approaches to Middle High German Literature,* **Göppinger Arbeiten zur Germanistik, 528 (Göppingen: Kümmerle, 1991).**

> Influenced by theoretical studies on women's literature, this collection of essays represents the first major attempt by American German medievalists to identify German medieval women writers and also to what extent women figured significantly in courtly literature. The focus rests on twelfth- and thirteenth-century authors and texts.

Dinzelbacher, Peter, *Mittelalterliche Frauenmystik* **(Paderborn, Munich, et al.: Schöningh, 1992).**

> After many years of intensive interdisciplinary research, Peter Dinzelbacher here presents a seminal monograph on medieval women's

mysticism. This study deserves particular attention because of the author's profound knowledge of the vast spectrum of women's mystical revelations. He deals with many women writers who wrote in many different languages during various periods, and who are still not studied enough by modern feminist medievalists. In German.

Dronke, Peter, *Women Writers of the Middle Ages. A Critical Study of Texts from Perpetua (†203) to Marguerite Porete (†1310)* (Cambridge: Cambridge University Press, 1984).
Dronke's seminal investigation of women writers of the Middle Ages opened the door to the highly exciting fields of medieval women's literature, gender studies, theology, and sociology. This book covers the vast spectrum from late antiquity to the early fourteenth century, focusing on Dhudoa, Hrotsvitha of Gandersheim, Heloise, Hildegard of Bingen, and Marguerite de Porete. Dronke also added a section with English translations of relevant text excerpts.

Ferrante, Joan, *To the Glory of her Sex. Women's Roles in the Composition of Medieval Texts* (Bloomington and Indianapolis: Indiana University Press, 1997).
One of the leading medieval feminists in the United States, Joan Ferrante here presents a vibrant and insightful interpretation of many different contributions by women to medieval literature, including the epistolary texts and mystical revelations, and she also explores how women were represented in courtly literature. Ferrante illustrates the extent to which medieval women could assume control of their lives and freely participate in public discourse by way of their literary productivity.

Gnüg, Hiltrud and Renate Möhrmann, eds., *Frauen, Literatur, Geschichte: schreibende Frauen vom Mittelalter bis zur Gegenwart*, 2nd, completely revised and expanded ed. (Stuttgart: Metzler, 1999; orig. 1985).
Individual contributors to this volume cover the periods in the history of German women writers from the Middle Ages to the present. The chapter on courtly women is basically the same as Ursula Liebertz-Grün's contribution to *Deutsche Literatur von Frauen* (see below). The second edition offers many new aspects, mostly with regard to modern writers, whereas the chapter on medieval women is almost the same as in the first edition. In German.

Hall McCash, June, ed., *The Cultural Patronage of Medieval Women* (Athens and London: The University of Georgia Press, 1996).
Even if women often had no real chance to contribute to the literary production of their time, many women exerted tremendous control over the production of literary text and artistic works through their patronage, as the contributors to this highly insightful collection of essays demonstrate. Unfortunately, German women patrons are not considered here.

Joldersma, Hermina, "Argula von Grumbach," *German Writers of the Renaissance and Reformation, 1280–1580,* **Dictionary of Literary Biography, 179 (Detroit, Washington, DC, and London: Gale Research, 1997), 89–96.**
Argula von Grumbach was a feisty and highly learned author of Reformation tracts and pamphlets fighting for the introduction of the Protestant Reformation in sixteenth-century Bavaria. This article provides a solid overview of our current understanding of Argula's contributions and sketches a biographical outline. All her relevant publications are listed.

Jones, Ann Rosalind, *The Currency of Eros. Women's Love Lyric in Europe, 1540–1620* **(Bloomington and Indianapolis: Indiana University Press, 1990).**
Whereas the translation of women songs in the present volume demonstrates for the first time that late-medieval and early-modern German women writers also participated in erotic love poetry, Ann Rosalind Jones produces convincing evidence that this was the case in contemporary English, French, Spanish, and Italian poetry, as well.

Klinck, Anne Lingard and Ann Marie Rasmussen, eds., *Medieval Woman's Song: Cross-Cultural Approaches,* **Middle Ages Series (Philadelphia: University of Pennsylvania Press, 2002).**
The contributors to this collection of essays examine a wide range of medieval women's poetry and study how women's participation in the culture of their time was portrayed in literary texts. They take stock of those literary genres in which female voices have traditionally been located, but they do not identify any new authentic poetic voice.

Liebertz-Grün, Ursula, "Höfische Autorinnen. Von der karolingischen Kulturreform bis zum Humanismus," *Deutsche Literatur von Frauen,* **Vol. 1:** *Vom Mittelalter bis zum Ende des 18.* **Jahrhunderts, ed. Gisela Brinker-Gabler (Munich: Beck, 1988), 40–64.**
This article offers a detailed discussion of medieval women's literary contributions and nicely summarizes current scholarship. First Liebertz-Grün focuses on the well-known French authors such as the *troubairitz,* Marie de France, and Christine de Pizan, then she turns to the significant fifteenth-century German writers Elisabeth of Nassau-Saarbrücken, Eleonore of Austria, Helene Kottanner, and Margaret of the Netherlands. In German.

Lundt, Bea, ed., *Auf der Suche nach der Frau im Mittelalter* **(Munich: Fink, 1991).**
From a highly welcome interdisciplinary perspective, the contributors to this volume examine the social, economic, and artistic conditions and possibilities for medieval women, explore gender specific functions and presentations of women, and analyze models of female existence. In German.

Rettelbach, Johannes, "Lied und Liederbuch im spätmittelalterlichen Augsburg," *Literarisches Leben in Augsburg während des 15. Jahrhunderts,* **ed. Johannes Janota and Werner Williams-Krapp, Studia Augustana, 7 (Tübingen: Niemeyer, 1995), 281–307.**

The topic of Rettelbach's article is Clara Hätzlerin's songbook, one of the major representatives of late-medieval Augsburg literature. He contextualizes her collection and examines the broad urban interest in traditional song poetry. In German.

Ruh, Kurt, *Frauenmystik und franziskanische Mystik der Frühzeit,* **Geschichte der abendländischen Mystik, II (Munich: Beck, 1993).**

Kurt Ruh, Nestor of medieval German scholarship, here presents an extensive and detailed overview of medieval German women's mysticism and Franciscan mysticism. This monograph stands out because of its in-depth analysis of the major mystical texts and the unmatched discussion of the historical-theological context. In German.

Smith, Lesley and Jane H. M. Taylor, eds., *Women and the Book. Assessing the Visual Evidence* **(London, Toronto, and Buffalo: The British Library, University of Toronto Press, 1997).**

Although paying little attention specifically to women in medieval Germany, the contributors to this volume provide highly insightful information about medieval women's relationship to the book as a cultural object, to book production, the role of women in manuscript illuminations, and about women's role as patrons.

Suppan, Wolfgang, *Deutsches Liedleben zwischen Renaissance und Barock. Die Schichtung des deutschen Liedgutes in der zweiten Hälfte des 16. Jahrhunderts,* **Mainzer Studien zur Musikwissenschaft, 4 (Tutzing: Hans Schneider, 1973).**

For a critical examination of German Renaissance and Baroque song poetry, one needs to consult the comprehensive monograph by Wolfgang Suppan. He offers a broad overview of the historical, musicological, and literary development of the *Lied*, and nicely contextualizes the major song writers, situating them in their social and cultural milieu. Suppan thoroughly outlines the historical development of the German song genre from the fifteenth to the seventeenth century. In German.

Tierney, Helen, ed., *Women's Studies Encyclopedia,* **3 vols. (New York, Westport, CT, and London: Greenwood Press, 1989–91).**

For concrete information about women from the earliest times to the present, both in the West and in the East, Tierney's three-volume encyclopedia meets a crucial demand. The articles treat their subject matter comprehensively without going too much into detail. This is also an excellent research tool with which to begin an investigation of medieval women's social, historical, religious, and literary functions.

Traeger, Lotte, "Das Frauenschrifttum in Deutschland von 1500–1600" (Ph.D. Prague, 1943).

Although mostly forgotten today, this doctoral dissertation represents one of the most advanced studies of early-modern German women's literature for its time and provides highly valuable information still not outdated. Traeger critically reviewed many of the early-modern women writers who are only now being discovered again by modern researchers. She was, however, not yet familiar with the women's songs contained in the present translation. In German.

Walz, Herbert, *Deutsche Literatur der Reformationszeit. Eine Einführung*, Einführungen (Darmstadt: Wissenschaftliche Buchgesellschaft, 1988).

This is one of the most detailed and comprehensive studies of German Reformation literature. Walz presents a vast spectrum of individual text genres and considers almost any text-type produced during the sixteenth century and relevant for literary-historical studies. Walz does not pay any significant attention to women's contributions to German Reformation literature. In German

Wilson, Katharina M., ed., *An Encyclopedia of Continental Women Writers*, 2 vols. (New York and London: Garland, 1991).

Wilson's encyclopedia offers an excellent and fast introduction to a vast number of continental women writers, from antiquity to the modern age. Each article provides a short biographical outline and a brief analysis of the most important texts. A short list of relevant research literature is appended to each entry.

Index

Library of Medieval Women

Christine de Pizan's Letter of Othea to Hector, *Jane Chance*, 1990

Writings of Margaret of Oingt, Medieval Prioress and Mystic, *Renate Blumenfeld-Kosinski*, 1990

Saint Bride and her Book: Birgitta of Sweden's Revelations, *Julia Bolton Holloway*, 1992; new edition 2000

The Memoirs of Helene Kottanner (1439–1440), *Maya Bijvoet Williamson*, 1998

The Writings of Teresa de Cartagena, *Dayle Seidenspinner-Núñez*, 1998

Julian of Norwich, Revelations of Divine Love and The Motherhood of God, *Frances Beer*, 1998

Hrotsvit of Gandersheim: A Florilegium of her Works, *Katharina M. Wilson*, 1998

Hildegard of Bingen: On Natural Philosophy and Medicine: Selections from *Cause et Cure, Margret Berger*, 1999

Women Saints' Lives in Old English Prose, *Leslie A. Donovan*, 1999

Angela of Foligno's Memorial, *Cristina Mazzoni*, 2000

The Letters of the Rozmberk Sisters, *John M. Klassen*, 2001

The Life of Saint Douceline, a Beguine of Provence, *Kathleen Garay and Madeleine Jeay*, 2001

Agnes Blannbekin, Viennese Beguine: Life and Revelations, *Ulrike Wiethaus*, 2002

Women of the *Gilte Legende*: A Selection of Middle English Saints' Lives, *Larissa Tracy*, 2003

Mechthild of Magdeburg: Selections from *The Flowing Light of the Godhead, Elizabeth A. Andersen*, 2003

The Book of Margery Kempe, *Liz Herbert McAvoy*, 2003

Guidance for Women in Twelfth-Century Convents, *Vera Morton and Jocelyn Wogan-Browne*, 2003

Anne of France: Lessons for my Daughter, *Sharon L. Jansen*, 2004

Goscelin of St Bertin: The Book of Encouragement and Consolation, *Monika Otter*, 2004

courtly love poetry (*Minnesang*), they do not offer significant innovation in style, imagery, or language, and do not reflect truly creative features in contrast to the works of outstanding contemporary poets such as Oswald of Wolkenstein (1376/77–1445), Hans Rosenplüt (ca. 1400/05–ca. 1460), and Michel Beheim (1416–ca. 1475). Max Wehrli curtly summarized the *opinio communis*: "The popular song was created by and for the lay people, and it is predominantly a secular song to be sung as communal entertainment."[59]

Several major themes in "Volkslieder" can be easily identified: a. the vast complex of love, sex, marriage, pregnancy, divorce, and violence; b. historical events; c. religion; d. riddles, jokes, and lies; e. dance and drinking songs; f. war songs (closely related to "historical events"); g. hunting; h. professional activities such as mining and agriculture; i. children.[60] Whereas courtly love poetry was primarily situated in the world of aristocratic ladies and knights, the "Volkslied" only translates, as Wehrli comments, the same themes and motifs, but develops them with a broader and freer context: "the courtly lady is transformed into the sweet, untutored girl; the sensory world is automatically woven into the song's content."[61]

Although most of these popular songs have come down to us anonymously, scholars such as Wolfgang Suppan, Hans Rupprich, Max Wehrli, and Peter Nusser have naïvely assumed that all poets were male. This traditional and rather unreflected attitude has been firmly cemented in reference works, encyclopedias, and handbooks on the history of German literature.[62] However, as our selection of secular love poetry indicates, rather the opposite appears to have been the case, although we need to examine each case carefully before we can reach definite conclusions.

Neither Elisabeth Borchers nor Marcel Reich-Ranicki live up to the expectations raised by the titles of their anthologies of German women's literature which suggest that a continuous history of female writing from the high Middle Ages to the present can be documented.

[59] Max Wehrli, *Geschichte der deutschen Literatur im Mittelalter: Von den Anfängen bis zum Ende des 16. Jahrhunderts*, 3rd ed. (Stuttgart, n.d. [1980], Stuttgart: Reclam, 1997), 1071.
[60] Lutz Röhrich, "Die Textgattungen des populären Liedes," *Handbuch des Volksliedes*, vol. 1 (1973), 19–35 (Section 2).
[61] M. Wehrli, *Geschichte der deutschen Literatur*, 1072.
[62] Among the many examples, see *Metzler Literatur Lexikon: Begriffe und Definitionen*, ed. Günther and Irmgard Schweikle, 2nd ed., rev. (Stuttgart: Metzler, 1990), 492f. only rarely do we find reflections about women authors. For German scholarship, see Albrecht Classen, "Frauen, Minne, und Gottesliebe: Rezeption von und Reflexionen über "Weibliches" in der deutschen Literatur um 1500," *KIn Vivia: Studies in Germanic Literature, Linguistics, and Culture* (Columbia, SC: Camden House, 1987), 88–90. here 89.